MY UNWRITTEN BOOKS

GEORGE STEINER

MY UNWRITTEN BOOKS

A NEW DIRECTIONS BOOK

Manufactured in the United States of America.
New Directions Books are printed on acid-free paper.
First published clothbound in 2008.
Published simultaneously in Canada by Penguin Canada Books, Ltd.
Designed by Rodrigo Corral and Gus Powell.

Library of Congress Cataloging-in-Publication Data

Steiner, George, 1929–
    My unwritten books / George Steiner.
        p. cm.
    Essays.
    ISBN 978-0-8112-1703-3 (cloth)
    ISBN 978-0-8112-1793-4 (paper)
    I. Title.
PR6069.T417M9 2008

824'.914—dc22

                    2007038256

NEW DIRECTIONS BOOKS ARE PUBLISHED FOR JAMES LAUGHLIN
BY NEW DIRECTIONS PUBLISHING CORPORATION
80 EIGHTH AVENUE, NEW YORK, NY 10011

CONTENTS

FOR AMINADAV DYKMAN, FOR NUCCIO ORDINE
— MORE THAN FRIENDS

Each of these seven chapters tells of a book which I had hoped to write, but did not. They seek to explain why.

A book unwritten is more than a void. It accompanies the work one has done like an active shadow, both ironic and sorrowful. It is one of the lives we could have lived, one of the journeys we did not take. Philosophy teaches that negation can be determinant. It is more than a denial of possibility. Privation has consequences we cannot foresee or gauge accurately. It is the unwritten book which might have made the difference. Which might have allowed one to fail better. Or perhaps not.

—GS
Cambridge, September 2006

| CHINOISERIE |

WHEN, IN THE LATE 1970s, Professor Frank Kermode, scholar and critic, asked me to contribute a study to his series of "Modern Masters," I proposed the name of Joseph Needham. Being neither a biologist nor a sinologist, neither schooled in chemistry nor in Oriental studies, my lack of qualification, the impertinence of my suggestion were patent. But I had long been spellbound by Needham's titanic enterprise and by his kaleidoscopic persona. Had there been a more learned, a more inclusive mind and purpose since that of Leibniz? What I had in mind was a possibly irresponsible approach to both the man and his works.

As a freshman member of the editorial staff of *The Economist* in London, I had been assigned to cover a public meeting in the cavernous St. Pancreas town hall. This meeting was in protest against the Anglo-American intervention in the Korean War. The arena was thronged. The chairman, a well-known left-wing publicist and fellow traveler, introduced Joseph Needham. The white-haired, somewhat leonine figure rose. He identified himself as the William Dunn Reader in Microbiology at Cambridge University and as a direct observer of conditions in both China and North Korea. He emphasized his virtually sacrosanct commitment to empirical and experimental evidence as a scientist of senior international standing. He then proceeded to hold up to the audience an empty shell casing. He assured his audience that this grim object provided incontrovertible proof of the use of germ warfare by American artillery. Needham and Chinese epidemiologists had checked and rechecked the facts. The chairman then invited the assembly to authorize a telegram of ardent revulsion to President Truman. But he also solicited anyone present who did not credit Dr. Needham's findings to have their say and state their dissent. The message to the White House would, in that case, not be unanimous.

There was no physical menace, such as there would have been in, say, a fascist rally. The chairman's offer was British fair play at its best. I was convinced that Needham was either self-deceived or lying for purposes of propaganda. But I sat motionless, mute. Not in fear, but under the physical pressure of embarrassment, numbed by the thought of making a spectacle of myself. Thus the "unanimous" protest was dispatched and communicated to the press. I left the rally utterly disgusted and depressed. At my lack of nerve and of courage (the German word is *Zivilcourage*). Not only has this episode, over half a century old, continued to weigh on me; it has oriented my entire attitude to those who flinch under totalitarian blackmail, be it National Socialist, Stalinist or McCarthyite. Be it that of the anarchist hooligan, the Maoist or the fascist. I knew from that evening onward how easily I would be prone to abjection.

Kermode sounded out Needham regarding my (impudent) project. To my surprise, Needham responded with an immediate summons. I met him in his master's office at Caius College. The room was magnificently crowded with books, offprints, galleys awaiting correction and a number of Chinese bibelots. If memory does not betray me, there hung in the corner both the master's academic robes and the surplice he wore when officiating and preaching in a nonconformist congregation outside Cambridge (a mission known only to his immediate circle and empowered by an immensely complex, idiosyncratic ecumenism). What struck me at once was Needham's palpable excitement at the prospect of figuring in the "Modern Masters" panoply. His "ancient glittering eyes" were indeed "gay" like those of the Oriental sages celebrated by

Yeats. His pleasure lit the room. I sought to detail my incompetence, to apologize for my amateurish intrusion into his compendious but also arcane orbit. Needham brushed this aside. He would inform and assist my portrayal. He would allow time-consuming interviews. We should initiate the project almost at once.

I then asked him about his testimony on germ warfare, on American bacteriological weapons and their use in Korea. I felt that I could not hope to undertake an introduction to his works, however inadequate, without knowing whether he believed that he had spoken the truth on this indictment. Whether he persisted in his claims to scientific objectivity. The temperature in the room plummeted. Joseph Needham's irritation, his anger were manifest. Even more so, the mendacity inside that anger. He gave no direct reply. It is said that those with a trained ear can detect the minute flaw in a crystal goblet when they pass their fingers across its rim. I heard this flaw, unmistakably, in Needham's voice. I sensed it in his posture. There could, from that moment on, be no realistic prospect of reciprocal trust. We did not meet again.

I never wrote the little book. But the wish to do so has stayed with me.

So far as I am aware, there is no definitive bibliography of Needham's *opera omnia*. The catalogue of lectures, articles, monographs and books extends well beyond three hundred. Their range is awesome. It comprises technical publications in biochemistry, in biology and comparative morphology, in crystallography by one of the ranking members of the Royal Society. There are voluminous studies, both monographic and summarizing, on the history of the natural sciences, theoretical and applied, on instrumentation and technology, from antiquity to the present. Like Bernal, whose reach was in some regards comparable, Needham wrote urgently about the place of the sciences in society, about the dangers posed by uncontrolled scientific progress and its exploitation for ideological and financial ends. The voice of the watchman, of the preacher rang loud.

Especially, Needham argued for the fostering of intellectual and political relations between East and West. He urged the imperative need for a "world cooperative commonwealth which will include all peoples as the waters cover the sea." In numerous texts, he expounded both the history and substance of the philosophy of science, with particular regard to Darwinian models of evolution on the one hand and schools of "vitalism" on the other. Possible analogies between thermodynamics and the chemistry of living organisms fascinated him. No less than Coleridge, a kindred sensibility, Needham challenged any dogmatic dissociations between organic and inorganic. He seemed to experience reality as an animate whole, interweaving matter and spirit. (What is there about Cambridge, an often gray, water-logged settlement in the East Anglian flatlands which, century after century, has inspired panoptic visions?) Time and again, Needham reverts to the vexed but profoundly creative conflicts between science and religion. He examines this dialectic in the light of socialist and communitarian ideals. Islam, every branch of Buddhism, Christianity and the history of doubt, of positive secularism are brought to bear on the debate. A closely-plotted paper on "The Limitations of Optick Glasses" is reprinted together with meditations on "Aspects of the World Mind in Time and Space" and on "Man and His Situation" (the Coleridgean confluence, again). Under a pseudonym, and unnoticed by most of his scientific colleagues, Needham has published historical novels dramatizing the fate and doctrines of radical sects during the Cromwellian period. But even this inventory, this *omnium gatherum,* to use Coleridge's macaronic tag, pales when set beside the monumental labours on *Science and Civilization in China,* an enterprise whose origins date back to 1937 and which has been carried forward beyond Joseph Needham's death in March 1995.

No bibliography, however, can convey the myriad-minded density of Needham's perceptions. Poetry, be it that of Tessimond or Blake, of Day Lewis or Goethe, of Latin hymns or of Auden, together with that of the singers and sages out of the Orient, is present throughout. The psychology of religious experience is exemplified by St. Theresa and Julian of Norwich, but also by Bunyan and by William James. Needham is a virtuoso of quotation. A citation from Thomas Browne's "flash of intuition" caps an analysis of Schrödinger and Max Planck on metabolism and irreversability. There is in Needham a poetics of technicality difficult to define. The historian of Islamic science, Said Husain Nadr, is yoked with Santillana in reference to that "desacralisation of Nature" which characterizes modernity, which has dominated the West after Galileo. C. S. Lewis on "the Abolition of Man," "a Christian inhabitant of what's left of Christianity," is set beside the pedagogic humanism of Master Kung.

The presence of Marx, of Marxist analyses, and of Engels's dialectic of nature is pervasive. Together with Haldane, Blackett, and Bernal, Needham belonged to a constellation of eminent British scientists of a Marxist, even at times Stalinist, persuasion. Economic depression in the capitalist order, blatant social injustice, the tide of fascism and Nazism in Europe, and Franco's victory in Spain generated enthusiasm for the Soviet Union. A fundamental concern, moreover, was at issue. The theoretical and applied sciences were in a phase of exponential brilliance; their development would soon modify every aspect of individual and social life. Yet the gap between science and a common understanding, between a scientific mandarinate and political awareness was growing alarmingly. To Bernal or Needham, it seemed evident that only a communist system such as was evolving in Leninism and Stalinism could bring the sciences into dynamic interplay with the intellectual, economic and political forces at large. Even the murderous follies of Lysenko's plant biology might have to be tolerated on the road to utopia. Marxism looked to be the inspired culmination of the threefold emancipation and rationalism generated by idealist German philosophy, English political economy and the French Revolution.

What was singular to Needham was his syncretism. Dialectical materialism "based itself on that very evolutionary progression which Spencer described with so much care." It can be shown, affirmed Needham, that "Marxism has Chinese roots as well as Christian ones from Neo-Confucian organicism through Leibniz and Hegel." Here, Needham's omission of the far more obvious pulse of messianic Judaism, central to Marx's angry genius and apocalyptic rhetoric, is arresting. Does it suggest a (rare) blind spot in Needham's omnivorous sensibility? It is, in any event, the Marxist reading of human history which underwrites Needham's unwavering creed: "However strong the forces of armed reaction, in the end progressive mankind has invariably found the strength to win the victory, and to preserve and develop the achievements of the human mind." This conviction gave to the sciences their unfolding logic. But it drew no less on radical political thought and on the visionary "futurities" eloquent in poetry. Blake and Shelley are as vital to Needham as Copernicus, Kepler and Darwin. The voices of the animate dead, be they those of poets, philosophers, theologians, economic and social theorists, pure and applied scientists, architects and engineers, crowd Needham's pages. His footnotes are a *summa* of the history of the mind. One can ask of Joseph Needham, as one asked of Leibniz or Humboldt: "Was there anything he hadn't read and read retentively?"

However unlikely the context—the metallurgy of gun barrels, the invention of noodles, the design of square sets for differential pressure gauges in mine ventilation—Needham's criterion is that of beauty, of effective comeliness. His pursuit is the one of symmetry, harmonic proportionality, of the interplay between logical priorities and structural variations. It is this pursuit which drew his sensibility most urgently to that of Chinese ideals and the harmonious dynamics of the Tao. Consider his paper on "The Earliest Snow Crystal Observations," published in 1961 in collaboration with Lu Gwei-Djen.

As in so many other instances, asserts Needham, priority of observation belongs not to classical Western antiquity but originates distinctively in East Asia. It relates to Chinese studies of solar halos and parhelia. Thus Chinese insights into the hexagonal and systematic configuration of snowflake crystals antedate by more than one millennium the erroneous conjectures of Albertus Magnus. Real understanding in the West dawns only with a brief Latin tractate by Johann Kepler published in 1611. Kepler's crucial intimations of harmonic relations in planetary orbits, moreover, are in their own neo-Pythagorean way kindred to Chinese feeling.

In classical Chinese texts, the number 6 is the symbolic correlation for the element "water." The hexagonal architecture of the snowflake was noted by Han Ying as early as 135 BC. Characteristically, Needham asks himself what kind of lens, what degree of magnification were available to the Chinese observer. It was the philosopher-sage Chu Hsi, "perhaps the greatest in all Chinese history," who related the six-pointed snow-flowers to the facets of certain minerals. The mineral invoked here is selenite, translucent hexagonal crystals of gypsum or calcium sulfate. As always in Needham, Blake's "holiness of the minute particular" radiates outward. The association of selenite with snowflakes is "exceedingly interesting because it prefigures the later development of the cloud-seeding process."

Thereupon arises the question which was to dominate, indeed to obsess, Joseph Needham's works and days. Having arrived at these brilliant empirical perceptions and interdisciplinary recognitions, far in advance of the West, why did the Chinese not press further? Instead, these matchless observers and makers of inwoven patterns were content to accept phenomena "as facts of Nature" and to explain them in "accordance with the numerology of the symbolic correlations." In Europe, after Descartes and the microscopic notations published in Robert Hooke's *Micrographia* of 1665, progress was swift. It led, inevitably as it were, to William Scoresby's orderly classification of the forms of snow-crystals, arrived at after his travels in the Arctic just before 1820. Why the difference? Needham's labors to answer this question will be monumental and heroic. The Chinese possessed the requisite means of magnification. But they chose not to press forward. Yet the very early, pioneering Chinese knowledge of the hexagonal symmetry of all snowflake crystals "ought to receive its meed of praise." That somewhat archaic, almost liturgical valediction is characteristic of Needham's idiom.

Or consider Needham's Hobhouse Lecture delivered in London in 1951. The topic is that of "Human Law and the Laws of Nature." The tidal argument begins with the *lex legale* and *jus gentium* as these are set out in Roman law. It takes in the trope of celestial legislation in the Babylonian creation epic and considers the "clearest statement of the existence of laws in the nonhuman world," which is to be found in Ovid's tribute to the teachings of Pythagoras. Characteristically, Needham cites Dryden's inspired rendition. The philosophy of law expounded by Ulpian and Justinian in turn leads to the seminal comparison with the doctrines of Confucius as these are set forth in Mencius. The category of laws of nature decreed, in the final analysis, by a suprapersonal, suprarational deity is implicit in the achievements of Kepler, Descartes, and Boyle. It climaxes in the divinely regulated cosmology of Newton's *Principia*. Chinese thought, on the other hand, conceives of "laws" in "a Whiteheadian organismic sense." Normative hierarchies and legislative patterns do pervade the totality of nature. But they remain essentially inscrutable and possess no "juristic content." This, concedes Needham, has distinct drawbacks so far as the evolution of modern science goes. But it avoided such inhumanities and hysteria as those manifest in European witchcraft trials and the capital sentences passed on animals. Needham's survey proceeds to Mach and Eddington and current theories on the status, experimental and ontological, of scientific laws. The concluding question is pure Needham. "Was perhaps the state of mind in which an egg-laying cock could be prosecuted by law necessary in a culture which should later have the property of producing a Kepler?"

No such *précis* communicates the art of Needham's presentation. Astringent technicalities alternate with horizontal vistas. Ironies sparkle. The basso profundo, however, is one of exasperated sadness. At perennial human cruelty and unreason, at the myopias which have inhibited different creeds and cultures from tolerant collaboration. I have adverted already to the great archipelago of Needham's footnotes. These constitute a counterpoint to the major narrative. They have a continuum of their own, spinning the argument backward and forward, sometimes subverting it with further qualifications and implicit challenges. Needham combines a certain baroque compendiousness, patterned on Burton, on Browne, on the seventeenth-century divines in whose stately rhetoric he is thoroughly versed, with the "plain chant" and directness of modern scientific papers. There is, perhaps, only one rival to his style. It is that of D'Arcy Wentworth Thompson's classic study of *Growth and Form* (Needham's contribution to chemical embryology is cited more than once). Consider Thompson on the shape of a splash, on patterns of growth in whales and turtles: "More curious and still more obscure is the moon's influence on growth, as on the growth and ripening of the eggs of oysters, sea urchins and crabs. Belief in such lunar influence is as old as Egypt; it is confirmed and justified, in certain cases, nowadays, but the way in which the influence is exerted is quite unknown." The voice could indeed be Needham's.

The seed from which the thirty tomes of *Science and Civilization in China* grew was sown in 1937. At that time, Joseph Needham was a research biochemist specializing in the study of embryonic development. His political sympathies were known to lie with the militant left then fighting in Spain. There arrived in Cambridge Lu Gwei-Djen. Needham was to marry her in 1939, two years after the death of his first wife, Dorothy Needham, herself a distinguished investigator of muscular biochemistry. Together with Lu Gwei-Djen came two other Chinese biochemists. "I found their minds were exactly like my own." This concordance posed the question of why modern science had not "taken off" in China. Needham, who had not mastered a single Chinese written character before the age of thirty-seven, addressed himself to the language and became quite fluent. It was an astounding accomplishment by a busy theoretical and experimental scientist already at home in a number of demanding tongues, including classical Greek and Latin. Subsequent visits to China and the pilgrimage to Cambridge of Chinese scholars soon confirmed Needham's somewhat legendary status.

During intervals of his work as a scientific consultant in wartime China, Needham conceived of a one-volume treatment of what was rapidly becoming a mesmeric challenge. By 1948, Needham had outlined seven volumes. These were to range from Chinese contributions to physics and mechanical engineering all the way to Chinese medical botany, navigation and physiological alchemy. Before long, the proposals for *SCC,* as it became known internationally, ran to ten monumental parts (some in double volumes). Soon even this manifold blueprint was overtaken by the plethora of new material and queries. The eighteen volumes which

Needham intended to write himself—several installments being simultaneously in the pipeline—would require an estimated sixty years of unbroken labor plus the immense task of preliminary research and bibliography. Literally hundreds of sources, many recondite and difficult to locate, would have to be combed. Needham was already forty-seven when he actually began writing volume one. His fantastically productive life did not attain the age of one hundred and seven necessary, according to his own calculation, to get the entire work done. He was still engaged with *SCC* two days prior to his death at ninety-four. Gregory Blue's bibliography records three-hundred and eighty-five titles, including more than one hundred and fifty scientific papers, a good many of substantial length and innovative significance. Prodigality did not cease during the composition of *SCC*. In range, in fruitfulness, Needham stands with Voltaire and Goethe. Like Goethe, moreover, he led an active public, political and academic existence while producing his magnum opus.

From 1949 onward, Needham delegated specialized subsections to an increasing team of collaborators. Over the following years, sixteen massive volumes were to be completed by fifteen experts, mostly though not exclusively recruited from China. Unavoidably, a certain gap began to open between the ageing magus and his younger auxiliaries. Ideological and technical differences arose. Some of these threatened to become fundamental. They bore on the particular constraints and "deep structures" of the Chinese language(s) in reference to a scientific worldview. Some of Needham's colleagues wondered whether the very concept of "science" in its Western sense could justly apply to the Chinese condition. Needham thought it fairest to engage in close and reasoned argument with his team. As K. G. Robinson points out, what was at stake were seismic displacements in the history and sociology of the sciences, movements which subverted Needham's cardinal ideal of "world science." Hence the two summarizing, retrospective and methodological sections of volume seven. Even within the Needham Research Institute established in Cambridge and pivotal to the encyclopedic enterprise, there were moments of friction. A number of projected rubrics had to be abandoned. Struggling against Parkinson's disease, fully understandable only to those closest to him, Needham strove to arrive at a conclusive statement, at a *summa* of his findings and convictions. He did not live to complete this task. The papers gathered in part two of volume seven do, however, come very near to it. They are unwavering. One last time, the hawk or, as Needham would prefer, dragon-kite, a Chinese contrivance, circles above a vast landscape of observation, scientific analysis, philosophic doctrine, and social thought.

I wish I had the competence necessary to pay due homage to the designers and compositors of the Cambridge University Press. Here is a saga in its own right. Experts have testified that no other printer and publisher could have satisfied Needham's requirements. On numerous pages, half a dozen languages and alphabets figure together with algebraic and chemical symbols. The visual impact alone is one of arcane wizardry. Chinese characters proliferate. Mushrooming footnotes pass from the chemistry of sealing-wax and the blowing of red glass in Nimrod's Babylon to Assyrian composites of lead oxide. These, in turn, direct the reader to technological treatises by two Western monks, Heraclius in the late tenth, Theophilus in the late eleventh centuries. Classical Greek characters, transcriptions from Arabic and Korean, lead a learned procession. Each tome comprises bibliographies and indices across a dozen tongues. Maps, astronomical charts, geometric diagrams, statistical tables, photographs of Chinese sites and reproductions of Chinese art abound. Russian sources are drawn upon. As are references to Indian mathematics and medieval alchemy. Worlds within worlds are brought to crowded life. Together with the three-volume *Principia Mathematica* of Russell and Whitehead, *SCC* embodies one of the high points in the history of typography, layout and publication. Both stem from the Cambridge University Press and, it is worth noting, precede the age of the computer.

Needham revels in putting forward what he takes to be Chinese precedence. Famously, this includes gunpowder, the manufacture of paper, printing with movable type, clockwork escapement mechanisms, the magnetic compass, porcelain, the invention of the stirrup and that of the waterwheel. But the catalogue, which runs to more than seven pages, also comprises less spectacular innovations and discoveries: the abacus, the cooling fan, collapsible umbrellas, firecrackers, folding chairs, moxibustion (a somewhat mysterious item), the toothbrush, the reel on fishing rods, our weather vanes and dozens more. Chinese observational astronomy and star charts, metallurgy, nautical techniques such as the sternpost rudder, hygiene, and preventive medicine were centuries, perhaps millennia, in advance of the West. As was Chinese anatomy, cartography and the equine collar harness with all that this device entails for transport. Long before the West conceived of such a tool, the Chinese were using hinged pistons in their forges and mechanical reciprocators for sifting grain. Their examination system for the selection and promotion of those highly educated officials who administered agriculture, the manufacturing industries, the mines and quarries, commerce on road and river across the vast extent and regional particularities of the Empire of the Middle, anticipated by more than one thousand years any comparable methods of recruitment and qualification in Europe. Chinese steam engines, affirms Needham, were puffing away many a long century before James Watt. Chinese astronomers had spotted novae and supernovae as early as 1400 BC. Add to all this metaphysical and cosmological constructs of incisive subtlety, aimed at articulating a coherent, equilibrated view of our universe and of man's place within it. This at a time when Western cultures were in essence rudimentary and plagued by irrationality.

Yet it was they who "broke through." It was Western science and technology, Western physics and engineering, which generated the planetary order in which we, the Chinese included, conduct our private and public modern lives. The high road led from Galileo and Kepler to Newton, Darwin, Rutherford, and Einstein. Not one Chinese name in that pantheon. It was Cartesian rationalism, Kantian criticism, Hegelian and Marxist scenarios of history which underwrote the exponential deployment of the Western understanding of and mastery over nature. It was as if Chinese science, so brilliant at dawn, had lapsed into a state of suspended animation till it could become congruent via, as it were, *force majeure*, with Western models and practices. Why this paradox of discontinuity? What could possibly account for this "cerebral arrest" (never, to be sure, total)? Possessed by this enigma, Needham time and again urged the question on his Chinese colleagues and collaborators, but most insistently on himself. It was more than an *idée fixe*. It incited essays, monographs, books of ever-increasing dimensions. By sensibility a polymath, one who took all knowledge and theory for his domain, a political-intellectual gadfly in perpetual motion, Needham found himself riveted to a central pivot. What explicable fatality, if indeed it was that, had lamed the initial, prodigal strengths of Chinese scientific and technological primacy?

"Voyaging through seas of thought" can be as combative as any saga. Needham wrestles with every available theoretical and interpretative model. For a time, analyses of a Marxist tenor, analogous to Karl Wittfogel's paradigm of "Oriental despotism" seemed decisive. Chinese historical and social constituents had evolved into a "bureaucratic feudalism." At first, this system fostered the cultivation of natural inquiry, of natural philosophy and technological appliance toward social benefits. Before long, however, it inhibited the rise of modern capitalism and of the scientific surge associated with it, most notably that of competitive investment. In contrast, the decay of European feudalism generated the new mercantile order. Thus, despite the superior rationality and social justice of the medieval Chinese order, the West, during the Renaissance, developed an exponential drive in both theoretical and applied sciences. This mastering impulse could flourish even under absolutist rule and in the face of religious censorship. In a word, perhaps socialism was the spirit of undominating justice imprisoned within the shell of Chinese medieval bureaucratism. If, however, Chinese civilization marked time in the past, the very elements which had caused this arrest might prove invaluable to the future. The Chinese ethos, opined Needham, its distrust of unbridled profit and entrepreneurial exploitation "may perhaps be more congruent with the scientific world cooperative commonwealth," which Needham envisaged as mankind's true future, a future which neither European nor North American mass-consumption capitalism could achieve. Yet coherent as it was, this diagnosis did not satisfy Needham (or his Chinese colleagues).

He felt compelled to look deeper. European historical, philosophical sensibility can virtually be defined by its trust in the originating, singular "miracle" of the genius of ancient Greece. Husserl and, in a qualified, revisionary way, Heidegger gave renewed vitality to this axiom. It is the merit of classical Greek thought to have privileged the pursuit of objective truths, of analytic-logical criteria in scientific argument, to have intuited the phenomenological primacy of mathematics. No other civilization crossed this threshold. Where else is there an Aristotle or a Euclid? Joseph Needham would not allow this apodictic, Eurocentric thesis. Nevertheless, he came to examine what might be contrasts of mentality—French *mentalité* is more precise—so radical as to weigh more than social or economic contingency. Whereas Bacon called for the extraction of experimental evidence from natural phenomena—an injunction in which Needham sensed the underlying analogue of torture and the fatality of appropriative violence—Chinese organicism sought to situate man within responsive harmonies far greater than himself, harmonies not to be "forced" or dissected. This stance might best be translated by Wordsworth's invocation of "wise passiveness." The very notion of sovereignty over nature, implicit in Western science and industry, was alien to the Chinese sense of the concordance and unison of the world. This hypothesis led Needham to propositions of a most dubious kind.

To him, the despotic primacy of the political in Mao's China signified that of "human moral values." Maoist dictates were meant to ensure the application of such values to "the health and well-being of your brother and sister at the bench, in the field, on the shop floor, and next to you in the office or at the council table." This Quaker idyll chose to ignore or even deny evidence of the atrocities of the Cultural Revolution, of the lunatic famine and miseries which Mao inflicted on his people—facts of which Needham had ample report—but also of that broad strain of cruelty, notably in regard to animal life or the incapacitated, which runs through the entirety of Chinese social history. When challenged, Needham would evade or denounce the question. Once again, there was the blindness or self-deception he had shown at the time of the charges of bacteriological warfare in Korea. Inevitably, Needham broke with a number of his peers and friends, withdrawing further into his sinological domain.

Reconsidering his lifework, Needham conceded that he had arrived at no firm, let alone determinant, conclusion. The pertinent factors were, despite the exhaustiveness of his survey, too manifold and complex. Even a vision as synoptic as his own could not contain them or give them probative status. He reviewed the evidence. China had experienced neither an Enlightenment on the European model, nor a bourgeois industrial revolution. Against these liberating though also ambiguous movements there militated a venerable centralized bureaucracy, cosmologically reinsured, and the stability (inertia?) of official and familial constraints. Needham discerned in Chinese consciousness a fundamental dissent from mercantile ideals, which, in turn, led to the failure to develop a "mathematically managed" economy. He allows the West might not have evolved its scientific methodologies without Euclid and Archimedes. Or perhaps the bourgeoisie could not have taken its seminal hold had it not been for the demographic and economic consequences of the Black Death. "These questions are stimulating, and sometimes provoke fresh thinking, but they have no definitive answers." There emanates from this magisterial postscript that particular honesty which attaches to defeat. Moreover, in the final analysis, what mattered to Joseph Needham was the instauration of a planetary network of collaborative scientific and technological progress in which a reawoken China would surely play a stellar role. Despite "Americanization" and the ravages of free enterprise, Needham would have welcomed signal aspects of globalization and planetary telecommunication.

In a ceremonial valediction deeply suggestive of Chinese rites (but also of Browning's "A Grammarian's Funeral"), Needham's coffin was carried around Caius Court, in the college of which he had been Master. The Fellows processed, two by two, following the coffin to the Gate of Honor. *Nunc Dimittis*. In homage to, in celebration of unrivaled labor, left appropriately yet also majestically incomplete.

I emphasize again my lack of competence in attempting to accede to this leviathan. Hence my possibly "illicit" approach.

It seems to me that it is not with other encyclopedic histories of science and technology that Needham's work can best be compared. It is with Proust's *Recherche*. *SCC* and the *Recherche* are, I believe, the two foremost acts of recollection, of total reconstruction in modern thought, imagination, and executive form. They are the two most comprehensive "architectures in time." They resuscitate a fantastically thronged and intricate past. They resurrect the past from the distortions and injustice of oblivion. There have been no more industrious archaeologists of consciousness. The hundreds of personae they summon back to felt life, their urban and rural settings, the multitudinous interplay of private, social, and natural agencies which they elucidate quicken into reality, into an inward empire as substantive, as tangible to our imaginings, as any in historical and literary narrative. (Both the *Recherche* and *SCC* can be "triangulated" in relation to Dante's *Commedia*.) Proust and Needham construct temporal epics of such detail and density, of such internal cross-reference, that they cohere. This ordered solidity, this compaction of internal echo and "crystallographic" structure, is difficult to define abstractly. Mandelstam on Dante may come nearest. But at whatever point you enter the Proust- or the Needham-world, its interior logic of relations, of point and counterpoint, is immediately sensible.

Each particle, each sheaf in the manifold harvest of resurrection is endowed with "a local habitation and a name," but also with reticulations so vital and extended as to interact with the surrounding plenitude. The text becomes precisely what China took itself to be: "an empire of the middle." In both cases, furthermore, in Proust's mosaic as in Needham's tapestry, the conventions of recognition and reference emerge, organically as it were, out of the process of composition (in neither magnum opus were the scale and labor predictable). All serious art and literature aims to generate its own specific design. It seeks to spiral back on its origins. In the *Recherche* this strategy is manifest. It is quite simply the subject of the work. In the long years devoted to *SCC,* the process of unfolding stylization, the elaboration of a distinction tone, were more gradual (the sum becoming collaborative), but no less dynamic. The "Needham effect" deepens from tome to tome.

Enter the edifice by virtually any of its myriad gates and the sensation of meshed unison, of harmonic reciprocities, is palpable. In 1086, Shen-kua clearly defines and calculates the degree of continental retardation, which is to say the constant interval between the theoretical time of high tides and the actual time in which they occur at any given place. A tide table is incised on the walls of the Chê-chiang pavilion, which stood on the banks of the Chien-Tang River. Needham invites us to compare this record with the thirteenth-century tide table for London Bridge. This is to be found in a manuscript now in the British Museum (Cotton MSS, Julius D,7). It is in September 1124 that Hsü Ching composes the preface to his account of an imperial embassy to Korea. Though not printed till 1167, this text reaches Korea. We shall meet its systematic information concerning tides again, in the rich context of the Chinese development of the magnetic compass (one of Needham's virtuoso demonstrations). Despite the tides of the Mediterranean, or perhaps because of their weakness, the earliest Western formulation of lunar influence does anticipate the Chinese. Needham plays fair. Among the earliest mentions is that in Herodotus. When "Tsou Yen was telling of the encircling seas, Pytheas of Marseilles at the other extreme bound of the Old World was experiencing the tides of the English Channel (c. 320 BC). Just at this time also sailors of Alexander the Great reach the mouth of the Indus near Karachi" (this "panning shot" is characteristic of Needham's technique). There, they are surprised not only by the tides themselves, but "by some kind of tidal bore." Like Ko Hung after him, Aristotle's pupil, one Dichearchos of Messina, conjectures that it is in fact the Sun which is in some manner responsible for tidal effects. Simultaneities or near-simultaneities across vast geographical spaces spellbind Needham even when they are premature or in part mistaken.

Just as during a Proustian soirée, personae make their entrances in the *SCC*; often we meet them again at other points in the intrigue. The cast is legion. Antigonus of Crasystos, the poet Mein Shêng, Soleukos the Chaldean, Poseidonius of Apameia, contemporary of Lhosia Hung. Alchemists, workers in bronze, admirals of far-flung explorations down the African coast, agronomists, mandarins and solitary sages in their mountain retreats. The Venerable Bede makes striking observations. Leonardo da Vinci goes completely awry. Meteorology and hydrology are leitmotivs. No Chinese meteorologist would have rejected, as did Galileo, Kepler's accurate intuition on the ground "that the moon could not have an effect on terrestrial events—such a view would have been contrary to the whole world view of organic naturalism." Nor must we forget that China possesses one of the only two great tidal bores or eagres in the world, on the Chien-Tang River near Hangchow (the other being at the northern mouth of the Amazon). "A thunderous noise is heard long before the bore arrives, and after it has passed junks proceed upstream in the strong current hardly under control." We see their bounding motion rendered in precise woodcuts. Proust takes us on local rail journeys, from hamlet to hamlet, each charged with its own poetry. Needham examines a Chinese world map of 1402 AD. On it the great bends of the Yellow River marked in white are plainly visible as is the serrated black line of the Great Wall. The large lake in Sinkiang may have represented Lop Nor. Arab-Chinese contacts involve explorers, cartographers, linguists. A world—part science, part fable—emerges out of time's mist as do the mountains and hermits in Chinese silk paintings. In c. 1150 AD, Abū 'Abdallāh al-Sharif al-Idrisi produces a global map for Roger II, King of Sicily. Neither Islamic cartography nor that of Chinese contemporaries takes into account the Earth's curvature. For al-Idrisi and his Norman patrons, China was still an unknown behind the Wall of Gog and Magog drawn on the map. But India and the East Indies figure. As do the "amoeboid" British Isles. At their uncertain left is the Island of Raslanda. Needham's imagination catches gentle fire. Perhaps this shape is meant for the Faröes; perhaps it is the origin of the mythical Isle of Friesland in the turbulent North Atlantic. Almost imperceptibly, Chinese mapmaking and land-surveying inform religious cosmography. They pervade the *Shen I Ching* (the *Book of the Spiritual and the Strange,* an apposite alternative title for *SCC* itself). In religious teachings, Mt. Khun-Lun is orbocentric. The stuff is that of legend, but it springs from the discovery of the process of the precession of the equinoxes by Yü Sung in his *Chhiung Thien Lun* (*Discourse on the Vastness of Heaven*) dated c. 265 of our era. In turn, Wang Chung argued that the sun's setting was only illusory "like the disappearance of the light of a torch carried by a man away from an observer on a level plane." The eminent Ko Hung will refute him. Proust seeks to metaphorize Relativity.

Or consider the account of sexual techniques in Taoism. Sources invoked by Needham comprise the *Book of the Mystery-Penetrating Master,* the *Immaculate Girl Canon,* the *Secret Instructions Concerning the Jade Chamber,* some of which still "circulate in the lending libraries of pedlars" (a notation which could include an entire novel). Chinese erotology was renowned. Complicated practices were developed "to preserve the seminal essence." Wise women such as Ko Hung and Tshai Nü play an important didactic role. Needham detects spoors of the influence and teachings of a coven of female magicians. Methods of coital retention point to a crucial doctrine in Taoist physiology. The spinal cord "was likened to the Yellow River in its downward-radiating trophic influence." All of which is allusively but precisely described in the *Excellent Jade Classic of the Yellow Court.* Most astonishingly, these techniques featured public ceremonies as well as the discretions of conjugal relations and private initiation. Our informant and witness is Chen Luan "the mathematician." A ritual dance took place by the light of either the new or the full moon. It mimed "the coiling of the dragon and playing of the tiger." After which, adepts enacted various rites of love in chambers alongside the temple court-yard. Analogies from the Western heritage spring to Needham's kaleidoscopic remembrance. He adverts to Longinus' *Daphnis and Chloe*, to Lucretius' dedication to Venus of his great philosophic poem. Footnotes grow tentacular, as did Proust's addenda and re-visions. They are vignettes at once haunting and erudite in their own right.

Astrology, "horary, judicial, or genethliacal" (Needham's lexi-con is a kingdom of its own) flourished. Intimately related to this pseudo-science was the determination of how to ascertain lucky and unlucky days. This strategy was by no means unique to China. Needham cites Babylonia and ancient Egypt, whence the expres-sion *dies Aegyptiaci* in the Roman calendar. The idea can also be found in Hesiod. "Until very recently, calendars produced in coun-try towns always marked lucky and unlucky days, and not many years ago the Academia Sinica itself began to publish rural calen-dars in order to attack the superstition and to impart elementary astronomical information." A footnote directs us to the difficulties which early friends of the Jesuit missionaries had in breaking away from this deeply entrenched superstition. Its survival, with vaguely Chinese resonance, among the New Age addicts and glit-terati of twenty-first century Manhattan would have amused Needham.

Frequently, he returns to his first love: "in studying the thought of the great Victorian, Henry Drummond, I found how liv-ing these ideas still are; love, he thought, might be considered the social analogue of the physical bonds which unite particles at the molecular level. And indeed in the history of chemistry the first understanding of chemical reaction involved the sexual analogy." Eros, the influence of the heavens, molecular biology—everything connects as it does in the hexagonal symmetry of the snowflake.

Observe the portrait of Wang Chieh in "the silver age of alchemy," itself an entrancing rubric. He was a secretive man versed in collecting the saliva of foxes. He exercised hypnotic powers. Essentially, however, he was a "level-headed metallurgical chemist" capable of producing such alloys as pinchbeck or golden-plated iron. Although Wang Chieh kept clear of entanglements with Taoist elixirs, he had to resort to mystification and charisma in order to attain and preserve his ranking position in the imperial maze. A century later we come across Lu Yu, author of *Notes from the Hall of Learned Old Age*. The Emperor was minded to bestow on deserving dignitaries golden Mandalas of the Numinous Empyrean. The metal had been transmuted by necromantic techniques. It was meant to provide talismanic safeguards against war, famine and other calamities. Yet just as the Court of Imperial Sacrifices was drafting the relevant edict, the barbarians attacked across the Yellow River. This was to be the death knell of the Northern Sung dynasty. (Cross-reference: that thunder of the guns at the approaches to Proust's Paris.) Confucuan rigor swept away the "magical nonsense" and Taoist liturgies of alchemical arts. Nonetheless, "if we now have powder metallurgy, beryllium alloys and liquid oxygen steel," this is owing to the wizards, not to the censorious apostles of common sense. Nor ought we to forget the occult women alchemists, such as the wandering poet Li Shao-Yün:

> The wind turns over the snow among the willow catkins
> And there are rosy clouds of peach petals on the water below.

"It is inspiring to realize that women have participated with men in the growth of the sciences from the beginning, from Mary the Jewess onwards." And how intriguing it is that adepts of Chinese medieval alchemy had a penchant just like their Arabic and European counterparts for riddling epigrams and gnomic sentences such as we find in the Hellenistic Corpus (and also in Goethe, fascinated by alchemy). After which Needham turns to a compendious survey of the transition from magic to modern chemistry and the Chinese synthesis of active insulin in 1965. A long, often winding road has led from the transmission of secret writings and the quest for elixirs of immortality in the third century BC.

Overarching this journey are the religious creeds, the philosophic schools, the ideologies of the Chinese past. Needham characterizes each in turn. There is Confucianism with its emphasis on the moral order of the universe and a corresponding social justice. Its pantheistic formulations are reminiscent of the "mystical rhapsodies to love" stemming from the pre-Socratics such as Empedocles and recurring in Orphic hymns. Confucianism offers among the most profound insights into the cosmic process of attraction and repulsion. But it allowed no room for science, only traditional technology. Its Taoist opponents, "irresponsible hermits" among them, developed "the only system of mysticism which the world has ever seen which was not profoundly anti-scientific." Taoism, as it flowered out of archaic roots of magic and shamanism produced a unique synthesis: "Taoism was religious and poetical, yes; but it was also at least as strongly magical, scientific, democratic and politically revolutionary." (Needham holding a mirror to himself?) The Tao enjoins a naturalistic organicism. It strives for a kind of "material immortality." The relevant terms are perhaps untranslatable. Taoism enjoins the perception that nothing is excluded from the reach of scientific inquiry, no matter how "repulsive, disagreeable or apparently trivial it may be." Yet its receptive passivity, symbolized by water and feminity, may have deflected Chinese wisdom from experimental science. "Sit down before fact as a little child . . . follow humbly wherever and to whatever abysses nature leads, or you shall learn nothing." Not a Galilean or Cartesian axiom. This invites an audacious supposition. Might it be that the dominance of Hebrew monotheism in Europe induced a rationalistic perspective on natural phenomena precisely alien to the Taoist abstention from trusting reason and logic? There is the challenging skepticism, the imperious demand for answers in Job. "But all such comparisons are unsatisfying and must remain mere suggestions for further thought." It may be that the deeper consonance is that between the Hebraic emptiness in the Holy of Holies and the emptiness in the last hall of the Taoist shrine at Heilungthan near Kuming in which there is a lone inscribed tablet with the characters *Wan Wu chih Mu*—"*Nature, the Mother of All Things.*"

Ancient China also fostered philosophic constructs per se. Among these the Mohists with their interest in scientific logic, science and military technology. Paradoxically, Mohist empiricism led to supernaturalism. So it does, adds Needham, in seventeenth-century Europe where belief in witchcraft attended on scientific rationality. More difficult to evaluate are the "Ming Chia" logicians, whose doctrines survive only in fragments. What is striking are the parallels between the conundra and antinomies propounded by these logicians and those famously argued by Zeno. There is, moreover, a temporal coincidence. Equally worthy of notice are the *Fa Chia* or Legalists. It is the "peculiar glory" of Chinese law—after the failure of the Legalists—to "remain indissolubly connected with custom based on what were considered easily demonstrable ethical principles": "the enactments of positive law, with their codifications, were reduced to an absolute minimum." Yet it may be that this very aversion from codification and positive law "was one of the factors which made the Chinese intellectual climate uncongenial to the development of systematized scientific thought." Once again, Needham reverts to the presiding question. And once again, he will find no demonstrable answer.

This "failure" however does not impair the status of his achievement. Which, as Laurence Picken put it, is "perhaps the greatest single act of historical synthesis and intercultural communication ever attempted by one man."

The question I wanted to pose is this: "Is *SCC* also something *else*?"

Am I implying that these thousands-odd pages of historical and analytic scholarship, that these bibliographies with their monographic dimensions, these hundreds of statistical tables, graphs, charts, maps, diagrams, and illustrations constitute what is in some manner a *fiction*? This conjecture may not be as demented as it sounds. During a brief spell of teaching in China, I asked distinguished Chinese scholars what they made of Needham's titanic labors. Almost without exception, they responded with a courteous, even reverent, yet also ironic smile (nuances of Chinese irony are manifold). Their appreciation of *SCC* was profound. How could it be otherwise? But no less profound was their astonishment at Needham's discoveries of Chinese priorities and scientific-technological accomplishments. How amazing, how gratifying it all was.

The demarcations between fact and fiction are subtly fluid. Always, the epistemological status of the two categories has been unstable. Proust's *Recherche* is charged with history. Be it in Herodotus or the most astringent of modern "cliometric" narratives, the combinatorial justification is that of style. Joseph Needham was possessed of a unifying revelation of exceptional conviction. Tidal motions of persuasion, minute details, came to cohere, as it were, from within. In turn, these energies of vision generated further evidence. *SCC* testifies to an organic unfolding of documentation, to internal patterns, of a scope which, as Needham persistently emphasizes, was undreamt of at the outset. Once tapped, the great current developed a temporal, a spatial compass which molded, which fertilized a landscape like no other. But the genius of the work is not in essence that of documentation and of inventory. Hence my amateurish intuition that a reader's best response is that assent to totality solicited by Balzac's *Comédie humaine* and, even more compellingly, by Proust. These "conceptual epics" create their own axes. The necessary response is one of trust, of richening at-homeness in an architecture and anatomy more alive, more authoritative than its multiple parts and perspectives. What Needham discovered he already knew to be there as do mathematicians and mystics. In his "China" no less than in his radical politics, utopia was concrete. He did not "make up" the story in any mendacious vein. But he "made it." Perhaps this helps explain both Chinese skepticism at so many of his findings and what now seems to be the isolation of Needham's immense atlas. Who reads it today? What continuum has it engendered?

The underlying paradox is that of Aristotle's famous proposition that fiction is "truer" than history. By which he seems to have meant that it is of a more incisive, representational generality, that it penetrates deeper into human motivations and experience. It is Shakespeare's "histories" which largely inform Britain's sense and readings of its own past. No formal history matches the veracity of Tolstoy's *War and Peace*. We are dealing not with archaeology but with "monuments of unageing intellect."

SCC, however, belongs to a more special genre. One that has not, so far as I can tell, been properly identified, let alone elucidated.

This genre dates back to Burton's *The Anatomy of Melancholy* (1621), if not earlier. It is a baroque species, a hybrid of minute erudition, arcane learning, esoteric citation and almost anarchic fantastication. Pedantry runs riot. But so does the allegoric, the emblematic, the stuff of dreams. The relevant texts share distinctive markers. They are polyglot, brimful of lists, catalogues, taxonomies. Learning—this is the key—is so detailed, so compacted, that it becomes autonomous. It breeds elaborations, edifices that exceed, by far, the immediate topic. It blends the technical fact with visionary possibility. Scholarship is so passionate, so "autistic" as to create monsters, both merry and menacing. Arcadias and nightmares are lit under the microscope. Baroque atlases, botanical dictionaries, zoological figurations are a graphic counterpart. In Arcimboldo, fruit and flowers are made human; explorers, cunning in navigation, report on three-headed tribes. The carapace is one of urgent knowledge. The magisterial, however, has, under pressure of its own volume, become surreal. Let me add three modern examples to *SCC*.

A. E. Housman's stature as classical philologist, textual critic and emendator was virtually unchallenged. Lesser scholars hesitated to publish lest he review their endeavors. The dismissals and castigations of Housman run a gamut of ironies as acerbic as Swift's. Soon these reviews developed a style of their own, more somber and unrelenting than Housman's poetry. One wretched editor of Juvenal "is seeking what he will never find, because it never existed"; a new commentary on Propertius misconstrues a key word, thus rendering the entire poem "shameful and ridiculous"; Dr. Postgate's conjectures on Aesop "are both sanguine and stubborn, and if once he gets hold of the stick by the wrong end he does not soon let go"; a suggestion in respect of Martial by Messrs Leo and Dau "is out of the question; it disregards Suetonius, it is violent in the extreme . . . it is metrically illegitimate." The more minute, the more technical the point at issue, the harsher Housman's reproof. It is this inverse proportion which takes on its own surreal intensity. Manilius' *Astronomicon* is of some interest to historians of ancient science. Its poetic merits are slight. Yet Housman lavishes on this text the full panoply of his learning. On every page of these tomes, the explanatory and philological commentary, itself in Latin, hugely exceeds Manilius's wooden verse. There have been suppositions that this mountainous labor, knowing itself to be unreadable, constitutes some opaque motion of self-punishment in Housman. The effect is at moments hallucinatory.

Vladimir Nabokov's contempt for the ignorance and vulgarity of the *profanum vulgus* matched Housman's. *Eugene Onegin* is not a very long work. Nabokov's translation, itself questionably pedantic, and commentary ramify to four volumes. Again, the philological apparatus and historical commentary are vertiginous. Every allusion in Pushkin, every derivation from French and English sources, every grammatical and lexical turn or possible crux, is subjected to voluminous exegesis. Previous commentaries and versions are treated with wolfish scorn. The "Notes on Prosody" amount to a monograph. There are encyclopedic excursions (*excursus*) on Russian diet, domestic habits, serfdom and the rules of dueling. Pushkin's contemporaries, the publicists and salons of the day, Czarist censorship, the erotica of the French libertines receive magisterial notice. But it may be that the truly surreal feature is that of Nabokov's one-hundred-and-six-page index. How many erudite witticisms and misdirections does it conceal? "Stalin (Once upon a time a turkey)." Housman the celebrated poet, Nabokov the lepidopterist and novelist of genius, sensing, ironizing the imp of madness in pure scholarship.

Mythologies of learning, black fables out of mandarin erudition inspired some of Borges's most memorable fictions: "Tlön Uqbar, Orbis Tertius," "Three Versions of Judas," "The Quest for Averroës," "The Aleph." Secreted codices, lost alphabets, the labyrinths of the Kabbala, imagined glossaries and pandects gather patient dust in "The Library of Babel." Borges abounds in absurdist classifications and inventories, some related to ancient China. Like Needham, Borges looked into the maelstrom of the fact.

I would have liked to explore further this genre, to locate *Science and Civilization in China* among these unicorns in the garden of reason.

Joseph Needham would not have approved.

| *INVIDIA* |

NOT MANY TODAY, I presume, read the works of Francesco degli Stabili, better known as Cecco d'Ascoli. What has survived of his writings are the incomplete epic *l'Acerba*, two astrological treatises, and a handful of sonnets, though here ascription and provenance are uncertain. On linguistic grounds alone, these vestiges are all but inaccessible to the common reader. Scholars interested in Cecco must study him either in problematic codices or flawed editions. Nonetheless, d'Ascoli's demanding, often rebarbative works have exercised their spell. Though strictly prohibited by ecclesiastical censorship—as many copies as could be hunted down had been consigned to the flames, and clandestine ownership brought inquisitorial pursuit—some fourteen fourteenth-century codices have survived and at least thirty turned up during the fifteenth century. What is held to be the first printed version of *l'Acerba* in 1473 is followed by twenty-six further printings between 1476 and 1550. During the sixteenth century, the theme which surfaces is that of Cecco's intellectual boldness, of an unyielding proto-scientific integrity which makes of him a true predecessor to Giordano Bruno and Galileo.

In his influential history of Italian literature, De Sanctis expresses qualified admiration for Cecco's uses of poetry to argue and impart scientific hypotheses, to aim for a synthesis between exact science and imagination in the manner of Lucretius. In his *Della varia fortuna di Dante* (1866–67), Carducci condemns Cecco's envy of the *Commedia*, an envy voiced by imitative malice. But he allows that d'Ascoli's didactic epic does exhibit flashes of cognitive and stylistic brilliance. A modern reading, such as that in Achille Tartaro's *Letterature italiana* of 1971, stresses the expository purpose of Cecco's astrological tractates. Tartaro locates Cecco's writings within the vexed context of Tuscan linguistic and literary hegemony and the uneasiness of the linguistic-psychological position of Bologna and the Marches caught between the prestigious polarities of Florence and Venice. A learned colloquium on Cecco took place in Ascoli-Piceno in September 1969. Its proceedings were published in 1976. These, too, are not easy to get a hold of.

More telling, perhaps, than this fitful legacy are three references. Petrach pays tribute:

> *Tu sei il grande Ascolan che il mondo allumi*
> *per grazia del altissimo tuo ingegno—*

where *allumi*, "to set alight," will take on hideous significance. The second is that of Leonardo da Vinci's use of Cecco's partially allegorical bestiary. And there is Goethe in act IV of *Faust* II:

> *Der Nekromant von Norcia, der Sabiner,*
> *Ist dein getreuer, ehrenhafter Diener.*

Elsewhere, Goethe, fascinated, as we have seen in regard to Needham's ancient China, by alchemy, salutes Cecco's intellectual courage and cites him as a daring questioner of both the heavens and the abyss.

Goethe's allusion to Norcia and the Sabine hills is to the point. No approach to Cecco d'Ascoli is valid if it does not reckon with his regionalism. Throughout the Marches, in the latter half of the thirteenth century, apocalyptic expectations, "*attesa dell età nuova,*" were rife. This wild country was often gripped by an intimation of the imminent collapse of the official *ecclesia* and its hierarchic ministry. Crucially, these intimations fed on archaic, on pre- and counter-Christian beliefs and rites. Heretical movements proliferated. They included the Zelanti or Spirituali, who had hived off from Franciscan orthodoxy. They numbered followers of the hermit Pope Celestine and his "grand refusal." The prophecies of the Sybil, also in dialect, were widely disseminated and eschatologically interpreted. They attached to certain numinous, haunted emplacements such as Mount Vettore and the dark Lago di Pilato. These mountainous corners are ghostly still. Magic, both white and black, sorcery, gusts of manic possession and of exorcism permeated daily existence in a landscape of lunar rocks, caverns, thick forests, and unplumbed lakes. To this day, local folklore and propitiatory rituals preserve traces of this uncanny heritage. As do colloquial rhymes:

> *Per l'anima de Cecco negromante*
> *che in una notte fabrico lù ponte.*

This motif of wizards capable of erecting a bridge in a single night via angelic or devilish dispensation is widespread throughout alpine and pre-alpine Europe. In the Marches, at every eerie or consoling crossroad, *magia naturale e diabolica* intertwine. In the *Atti* of the 1969 *convegno,* Febo Allevi provides a masterly survey.

Despite arduous ferreting in the archives (hope persists), hardly any aspect of Francesco Stabili's life and catastrophe remains either clear or uncontroverted. His date and place of birth are conjectural. Ancarano in 1269 looks likeliest. But Giovanni Villani's *Cronica* and the material gathered by the antiquarian Angelo Colocci, our principal sources, give only sketchy, belated information. What is believed to have been the only authentic portrait of Cecco vanished from Ravenna in 1692. Did the Devil make off with it? Nothing is known of Cecco's childhood or upbringing. Schooling was in the hand of monasteries. Somewhere along the way, d'Ascoli acquired his considerable knowledge of Latin and neo-Latin together with his familiarity with classical poetry and mythology. Fragmentary indications point to his studies in Ascoli and Salerno, a politically battered but not undistinguished center of advanced learning. Whether his *cursus* included a stay in Paris, center of scholastic cosmology and disputation, is altogether uncertain. (Did Dante visit Paris, as some biographers insist?)

At an early age and under circumstances unknown, Cecco d'Ascoli was appointed to the chair of astrology at the University of Bologna, *alma mater* of all Western universities. What few facts have come down to us do not make much sense. This nomination, usually dated 1322, seems to have involved a vote by the students. Cecco's popularity, his flamboyance, seem to have provoked officious jealousies among his colleagues and ecclesiastical authorities. He was indicted for professing *"cose vane e contra fede"* by the Dominican Inquisitor Lambertus de Cingolo on December 16, 1324. Cecco was compelled to leave Bologna. We know nothing of what is said to have been his reelection to his professorship " by the acclamation of the students." When d'Ascoli surfaces again, in late May 1326, it is as court astrologer and physician to Duke Carlo of Calabria, then regent of Tuscany. Under his patronage, Cecco may have thought himself immune to ecclesiastical censorship and persecution. He indulged in philosophic-scientific speculation, prophesied and cast horoscopes, perhaps unguardedly. Arrested in July 1327, Cecco—Francesco degli Stabili—was burned alive together with all his works between the Porta a Pinti and the Porta alla Croce in Florence on September 16th. The sentence was carried out under the authority of the ducal *Vicarius,* one Lord Jacob of Brescia. Hagiography has it that Cecco went to his death proclaiming "I have said it, I have taught it, I believe it." This may well be a post facto romantic embellishment. But what explains his appalling fate?

Conjecture has been rife. That Stabili was a proud, irascible, arrogant, possibly disturbing and self-advertising individual is reflected in available testimony. He made dangerous enemies with abandon. He shone on the precarious margins of official academic and ecclesiastical tenure. He drew on the fitful support of students and absentee princes. This somewhat histrionic *"piromanti, geomanti, negromanti, idromanti,"* which is to say magus of the four elements, trod on too many toes. What, however, justified a charge of heresy? The Holy Office records of Cecco's trial and capital sentence *may* indeed be preserved in Rome. Certain scholars have thought so. If so, however, they have not to this day been made accessible let alone published. What can we glean from *l'Acerba*?

D'Ascoli's magnum opus poses nearly intractable problems of a linguistic and hermeneutic order to even the most qualified of medievalists and historians of science. Its very title has been diversely read. Does it derive from Latin *acervus*, signifying an assemblage, a congeries of disparate components? There is warrant for this usage in Cicero, Virgil, and Quintilian. Or, more plausibly, does it refer us to Latin *acerbus* meaning "harsh," "unripe," "incomplete"? Such asperity would be modeled on the style of Suetonius and Lucretius, though the truest parallel seems to me to be that with Manilius's *Astronomicon* (shades of Housman). Who chose this title in the first place? Was it a covert hint at the work's tragic incompletion? The idiom of Cecco's astrological-cosmographic epic bristles with terminological singularities and etymological hybrids. It has been described as a parlance often specific to its author or locale, a *lingua picena* spangled with particles of colloquialism and dialect. It matches the motley and idiosyncracy of its tragic begetter. At the time, the Italian linguistic condition was one of assertive regionalism and polyphonic rivalries. Latinate borrowings, scarcely integrated, strains of Provençal, of Sicilian, of French enter the crucible of *l'Acerba*. But so do echoes of Arabic, so ubiquitous across Sicily and Calabria, and so instrumental in the development of astronomy. Together with the technical, often deliberately occult vocabulary, is the *parlande tacendo* or "silent speech" of medieval medicine, alchemy, prognostication, and allegory of the most convoluted kind. An early Latin commentary, printed in 1501 and covering only the first part of Cecco's poem, seems to make matters worse.

But the question remains. What heresies, if any, can be extracted from *l'Acerba* and the two astrological treatises? Cecco can be interpreted as saying that Christ was subject to astrological determinism. Even God the Father, one or two passages intimate, cannot alter the course and laws of nature (Aquinas would have agreed). Yet elsewhere, d'Ascoli explicitly postulates free will. Might there be heterodox elements in Cecco's commentary on Giovanni di Sacrobosco's (John of Holywood's) highly influential, almost canonic, *De Sphera mundi*? Can Cecco be taken to argue that celestial spheres emit malign, demonic agents whom magi could, under certain hermetic circumstances, command to do their bidding—the Faustus theme? Was there in d'Ascoli, as in Needham's Taoist sages, a "magic materialism," a recurrent positivism in regard to the human person in its cosmic context? "The human body was never divine." Only the intellect can and must prevail:

> *Intendi e vedi con la menta a scienzia*
> *Che mai l'eterna beata natura*
> *Sena ragion non fece creatura.*

Yet despite these Aristotelian rather than strictly Thomist foundations, Cecco's vision emphasizes the limits of rational perception and the boundaries which separate the natural from the supernatural. At no point, as Thorndike shows in his august history of medieval magic and science, do Cecco's speculations exceed in unorthodoxy those of eminent contemporaries, such as Albertus Magnus. On learning of Cecco's death, and with a clear hint that he had been entrapped in rivalries between monastic orders, Pope John XXII, out of Avignon, remarked: "The Minorities have lost the last prince of the Peripateticians" (of philosophers of a truly Aristotelian provenance).

What other motives could there have been to account for the Inquisition's hounding and condemnation? (By 1707, a Jesuit scholar will acclaim Cecco's astrology.) Rumor had it that the master had cast Christ's horoscope. This virtuosity may have been blasphemous, though the issue is not clear. More mundanely, d'Ascoli appears to have incensed his ducal employer by preparing and making public a horoscope which foretold the ill fortune of the Duke's daughter, the future Queen Joan (prediction was always a dangerous art). All this, even if it is so, does not explain adequately Cecco's repeated persecution and indictment first in Bologna, then Florence, or his death. Thorndike's finding stands: until new documentary evidence turns up, the whole matter remains obscure and even mysterious.

One stubborn theme, however, is recurrent, right from the start:

> L'invidia a me à dato sí de morse
> Che m'a privato de tutto mio bene.

Invidia eresiarca, livore invidioso—references to, invocations of "envy" are constant. He underlines them himself, as do his contemporaries. The reflex is twofold: *invidia* stalks the magus who is, in turn, charged with fierce envy, which he manifests to others. In his inspired fresco of the Last Judgment in Santa Croce in Florence, Orcagna depicts the *poeto-mago* among the damned. *Invidia,* virtually incarnate, bearing its green mask, hounds Cecco d'Ascoli's works and days.

This ground-bass hums, as it were, around the topic which has in fact kept Francesco Stabili's name from oblivion: that of his relations to Dante. Once more, the evidence is opaque and, at several points, contradictory.

Already during his lifetime, d'Ascoli was regarded as a contemner of Dante, as one lacerated by envy of Dante's supremacy and of the fame Dante's writings enjoyed. From Venice, Giovanni Quirini blesses Florence for having assuaged Dante's offended spirit by consigning Cecco and his labors to the flames (nevertheless, he begs for a clandestine copy of *l'Acerba* if any have survived). An early play on words blames Cecco for being *cieco* (blind) to Dante's obvious preeminence. Carducci echoes this view when he classifies *l'Acerba* as a frustrated imitation of the *Commedia*. Hence, argues Carducci, the choice of the *doppia terzina* as its stanzaic form. Moreover, are there not in this gnarled opus two stanzas which explicitly vituperate Dante? Other commentators argue for a literary and doctrinal basis to Cecco's alleged jealousy. Cecco's rude style is meant to countervail Dante's lofty, even pompous eloquence. It speaks truth. With his *De Monarchia,* Dante incurs ecclesiastical displeasure. He is, at one stage, suspected of alchemical and divinatory practices. But he solicits and finds adroit accommodation with the church and its monks. *L'Acerba*'s treatment of cosmology is "scientific," it takes speculative risks. Dante enlists liturgical safeguards and irrational ecstasy. Or was there some hidden polemic at issue?

Luigi Valli's *Il lingiaggio segreto di Dante e dei "Fedeli d'Amore"* was published in Rome in 1928. It claims that Dante, Petrarch, Francesco de Berberino, and Cecco himself belonged to a hidden sect which worshipped a feminine incarnation of holy wisdom, of Sophia. Such covens were not infrequent at the time. Communicating among themselves in code, cultivating links with Templars and Ghibelline (pro-imperial) factions, these adepts gloried in the symbolism of the mystic rose. In turn, this symbolism drew on Islamic and Persian mysticism, diffuse in learned circles, together with kabbalistic touches. Dante, so argues Valli, broke with the

"Faithful" and sought understanding with the Guelph (pro-papal) potentates. Worse than that, especially in the eyes of a misogynist such as Cecco, the cult of Beatrice and the florid Mariolatry of the *Paradiso* represent an unforgivable betrayal of Sophia, herself an abstract and secret concept.

Not only is the evidence for any of this tenuous in the extreme, but the texts we do have provide a very different perspective. Today, the majority of qualified exegetists consider the two stanzas in *l'Acerba* which assail Dante to be later, spurious insertions. The echoes of the *Commedia* in Cecco's poem are undisguised and positive. Thus, Section XVI in Book II looks admiringly to *Purgatorio* XVI. Furthermore, there is more than one hint that Cecco d'Ascoli deemed Dante's exile and threatened fate—he was to be burned alive if he returned to Florence—to be symmetrical with his own.

And yet: Gianfranco Contini, whose ear for the pulse of intent in poetry is well-nigh flawless, does define *l'Acerba* as "an anti-*Commedia*." The shadow of *avara invidiosa,* the phrase is Cecco's own, continues to fall.

What is it like to be an epic poet with philosophic aspirations when Dante is, as it were, in the neighborhood? To be a contemporary playwright when Shakespeare is out to lunch? "How can I be if another is?" asks Goethe. Outside my door at the Institute for Advanced Study in Princeton I heard J. Robert Oppenheimer fling at a junior physicist the demand: "You are so young and *already* you have done so little." After which, the logical option is suicide. Themes of rivalry, of jealousy, of envy have been perennially cited and dramatized. They are as ancient as Saul's rage over David's meteoric ascent and the venomous derisions spat out by Homer's Thersites. Salieri's murderous jealousy of Mozart, probably fictive, has been set to music, staged, screened. What of Iago and

Iachimo—the diphtong *ia* does seem to grate on Shakespeare's nerves? Or those condemned to play against Roger Federer at Wimbledon, year after hopeless year. Green, the color of springtime and ripening is also that of *invidia* and of bile (one can taste envy in one's dry mouth). Did Iscariot hasten into the night of infamy because Jesus had clasped another disciple to his bosom? The symbolic scenarios, the allegories, narratives, the exercises in moralistic correction, are innumerable.

There is hardly any mythology or cultural archetype in which Cain, arbitrarily, incomprehensibly disadvantaged, does not seek out Abel. Rome is grounded on fratricidal jealousy. The *moralistes* of the seventeenth and eighteenth centuries took particular note of envy and of the mundane hypocrisies which cloak it. Montaigne had preceded them, as had Juvenal and Martial before him. But we lack a philosophic exploration, a phenomenology in depth of envy. It is the painters of emblems and allegories who have come nearest. The subject is close to being taboo, to bordering on the excremental, as Swift intuited. The honesty, the probing within the open wound of the self, hurt too much. The savor which surfaces from the recesses of the ego is too fetid to breathe. Perhaps, although we cannot really imagine this, the torture of the fire which Cecco d'Ascoli experienced was not the worst he had endured.

The Hebrew Bible tells of a "jealous" God, though our epithet may not render the polyvalent connotations of the original. There are indices in the Books of Moses and the Psalms that He is jealous of the lesser, but more ancient deities whom He has overcome. The affair at Babel does suggest that God is jealous of man's heaven-storming skills and political organization. Euripides's intimations are subtler and more disturbing. In essence archaic and not long enfranchised from chaos, the gods come to apprehend and, it may well be, to envy the ethical refinement of mortal men and women. Mortals have evolved, reproachfully, beyond the primal furies and quid pro quo of the Olympians. Witness the indictment of divine puerility in the *Hippolytus* and, incomparably urged, in the numbing albeit fragmentary close to the *Bacchae*.

Usually, however, the dialectic tilts the other way. It is man who is envious of the deities. Who envies their powers, beauty, erotic license, and, principally, their immunity to death. Homeric gods can suffer wounds, but these heal on the instant. It is mortals who feel unjustly done by, hammered, patronized by God or the gods. With revealing passion, Milton modulates this feeling into Satan's bitterness at what he deems to be Jehovah's unfairness, his favoritism and gratuitous discriminations among angelic orders. Satan exhibits a self-justifying envy and jealousy of the Son so consuming that it burns hotter than the flames of damnation. It is the "humanity" of his emotion which makes him so seductive to our sensibility. The resultant defiance is an archetypal conceit. The giant warrior against Thebes, Capaneus hurls insults at Zeus. His "great shade burning still," he will not refrain from doing so even in the pits of Dante's *Inferno*. Marlowe's Tamburlaine finds it intolerable that any power exists superior to his own:

> I hold the Fates bound fast in iron chains,
> And with my hand turn Fortune's wheel about,
> And sooner shall the Sun fall from his sphere,
> Than Tamburlaine be slain or overcome.

This complex, dramatized in the plot of the titans and of wars in heaven, has, in a forceful cliché, been called "Promethean." If it articulates mutinous envy, it also poses the perennial challenge of theodicy. How can an omnipotent deity have created in its own image—an exceedingly obscure, almost taunting notion—a being too feeble to escape affliction, misery, temptation? What sadistic experiment or game is being played? May the Almighty be cursed for his pains, in all senses of that word. On the heath in *Lear*, on the barrens of Jutland from which Kierkegaard's wretched father blasphemed, the gods torment and kill us "for their sport." We did not ask to be born.

Invidia between creator and creature can be directly competitive. Mythologies, so often a shorthand for logic, bear witness. A lighthearted maiden boasts of spinning a web more delicate, more prodigal of adornment than any Athena can weave. She is turned into a spider. Apollo flays alive his rival in the mysteries and performance of music (Titian's *Marsyas* enacts every nuance and torment of vengeful envy). Inevitably, the *agon,* the duel, is reciprocal. The human creator senses that his achievements, however exalted, fall short of what is set out in the natural, which is to say divinely engendered, world. The unfathomable lineaments of this encounter are to be found in Job. God's answer to His suffering servant, God's apologia for the gratuitous horrors He visits upon him, is emphatically esthetics, dare one say "Neronian." It is the boast of the master builder and supreme artisan. Man cannot match, let alone exceed, the power, the fantastication, the awesome loveliness out of God's workshop. What are our sublimest paintings when compared with dawn? Our music when set beside that of the celestial spheres? The *Paradiso* is the classic statement of these incomparabilities. Man's only, but indestructible, counterstatement is that of the words, of the grammar in which Job is set down. A language God *must* speak if He is to be heard. Strikingly, this intrigue of mortal questioning and challenge, always frustrated, endures long after the eclipse of classical myths and scriptural authority. Surrealism is at once a parody of and alternative to given reality, to the tedious economy of reason. Its atheism is one of nervous subversion. It can do better than a dead God. Among the most fertile of modern makers we find the theme of God's jealousy and of the writer's or artist's provocative defiance. Tolstoy was dubious of his own mortality. He went into the forest to wrestle with that "great bear" who might not have been capable of begetting Natasha or Anna Karenina. Picasso adduces the rival creator in the next room. "It is not for God's honor that I have painted this chapel," says Matisse at Vence, "it is for my own." A deep-rooted ambivalence is in play. Also the human creator can grow jealous of his creatures, of the complex dynamism by which they threaten to become autonomous, to elide his purpose and control. He may feel tempted to pulverize what he has crafted. Writers, composers, artists have been known to destroy their own works, for reasons entangled in the roots of creation. Or to wonder whether what they have molded, composed, verbalized outstrips any conceivable transcendent model. What does God make of Hamlet or Cordelia, what is His honest opinion of a Bach Passion or the *Missa solemnis,* where it is often masterpieces conceived in his honor which pose the most acute challenge? (Could it be that Shakespeare's famed abstention from any verifiable religious stance relates closely to the condition of his own creativity?)

In a mundane setting, the wellsprings of envy are multiple. None more corrosive than a perception of injustice. The rewards for my labors have been bestowed on another. My contributions have been passed under silence whereas self-serving mediocrity or even plagiarism have been glorified. Informed by prying paparazzi that the Nobel had gone to a far lesser man, the finest of living Italian poets burst into helpless tears. Unfairness can attend on birth. "I was born ugly or even impaired; he is made handsome, Apollonian, charismatic," where beauty in men can be an especially unsettling provocation. "The social, material circumstances have been against me from the outset." The Alighieris belonged to a Florentine elite. They afforded Dante a choice schooling and entry into civic dignities. I, Cecco, have clawed my way out of poverty and sub-literacy in a provincial nest. "Mute, inglorious Miltons" have been rendered so by racial discrimination, class prejudice or the millennial constriction of women. Inexplicable hazard has snatched the laurels from me, consigning me to be one who "also ran." "It is not enough to be a good general, one has to be a lucky one," so Napoleon. Where "luck" signifies the elusive gremlin, the satyr-play which underlies high drama. The ancients erected altars to indecipherable Fortuna. "Had I looked more closely, more confidently at the X-ray diffractions which two ruthlessly ambitious competitors seized upon, it is I who would have published the key to molecular life and received the trophies which followed." One looks back, in unhealed hurt on the moment, on the deflection in which the decisive chance was missed. The sense of an irreparable lack of fair play on the roulette of good and ill fortune can breed venom. Men have betrayed, committed perjury, plagiarized, even murdered out of *invidia*. The fortunate rival is close by, making detestation the more choking. When one meets his cordiality, his barely disguised compassion in the office, in the laboratory, in the regimental mess or the literary garden party, cordialities can turn to vomit. The more defined the relevant milieu and its hierarchies, the more acid the taste. Poe was a penetrating observer of this concatenation.

Elsewhere, I have tried to analyze the tensions between teacher and pupil, between masters and disciples with their inescapable potential of psychic castration. The simultaneity of pride and jealousy on both parts makes the relationship in some sense contradictory. Operative is the notorious double bind. As he imparts his knowledge, his skills, the master expends himself and diminishes his means. Time is against him. On the other hand, it is the apprentice's progress, the nurturing of the student's capacities which constitutes the explicit aim and renown of the pedagogue. The more evident the transfer of skills, the greater the merits of the coach. Yet the more acute the danger that he will be made redundant. A dialectic at once positive and self-destructive. For his part, the learner celebrates the accomplishments, the prestige of his instructor. He or she will often, be it unconsciously, mimic the master's gait, his diction, his brush stroke or touch on the keyboard (imitations of Oppenheimer's mannerisms were rife in Princeton).

In farewell, he will proclaim to the vulgar world: "This is our master, famous calm and dead, / Borne on our shoulders" (Robert Browning). Yet at the very same time, the disciple, the apprentice, the tyro in the master class strives not only for emulation. Inherent in the process of pupilage is the drive to supercede. The master is not only to be accorded his school and legacy. He is to be surpassed. Nowhere is Freud's dramaturgy of the Oedipal more graphic. The paternal, magisterial figure is to be outgrown, and in the logic of the situation, destroyed. For his part, the teacher in the music room, in the atelier, in the writers' workshop, in the laboratory, is aware of this ultimately ruinous challenge. Indeed, he must foster and encourage it, as does Zarathustra. He must acquiesce and glory in his own relegation. Both parties are thus *en fausse situation.*

In the fine arts, in the composition and execution of music, this fatality is perennial. The ageing, illustrious painter assigns to an obscure apprentice the design of an ancillary, marginal figure in his fresco. Verrochio glances at the result and looks on Leonardo. He confronts a death sentence, his works now consigned to obsolescence. The esteemed teacher and executant in the music academy hears, perhaps through a door left open by chance, the improvisations of a recalcitrant student. He is listening to the intolerable Glenn Gould. On the instant, his ear takes in the eclipse of his own attainments, the quantum leap into another performative dimension. With luck, his name will survive as a footnote in the biographies of a genius. Hired, compassionately, to assist in, to verify his own lifework in astronomy and celestial mechanics, the starved *famulus* (one Kepler) not only solves hitherto intractable problems but topples Tycho Brahé's entire cosmology. In turn, each initiate in the original psychoanalytic tribe breaks away in aggressive rebellion, setting up rival constructs and therapeutic methods. Hence Freud, the father-founder's grim self-identification with Moses. In the history of philosophy, parricide is of the essence. Aristotle must turn on Plato. Sequence turns to critique and repudiation. The *Assistent,* in the German academic usage, sets out to undermine, to deride the teacher to whom he owes his own advancement. Heidegger's treatment of Husserl provides an odious example. Until recently, this configuration was rarer in literature, where any formal instruction was exceptional. Now, with the proliferation of "creative writing" programs and workshops, it will become routine. What is the instructor, more often than not of the second rank, to make of a student's inspired manuscript?

The existential consequences can be, they often are, close to pathological. The master can seek to deceive his disciple, qualifying his work as a failure, discouraging him from further pursuit. Arts and music are replete with such episodes. Competitions, the award of bursaries and vital preferment can be used to humble, to lame a threatening upstart. The excessively talented or ambitious can be snuffed out by a dismissive book review or a negative confidential reference. This vulpine tactic, not always innocent of sexual pressure or insinuation, was often enlisted against gifted women. Reciprocally, the student, the trainee who has the incomparable advantage of youth on his side, can demolish his or her teacher, surpassing his mastery and consigning his ideals to the past. Ridicule, in the hands of the young, is a ferocious weapon. It helped destroy Adorno. It flowered in the graffiti produced during the student insurrections of 1968: "No more masters. Let the dying teach the dead."

An authentic teacher—they are not thick on the ground—will not envy his more talented, more creative student. He will, in Wittgenstein's parable, bid him "knock away the ladder" by which he has led him upward. He may even abdicate from his own role and vocation when a young Newton enters his lecture hall (this move is reported of Isaac Barrow). He or she will recognize, albeit with a certain sadness, that it is a teacher's supreme reward to have trained, to have spotted and inspired those who will soon surpass him, whose compass and celebrity will exceed his own. In my fifty years of teaching, I have had four pupils, three men and a woman, abler, more original, more open to crisis and modernity than I am. Two, on political and psychological grounds, turned on me. They held up my own work to derision. One has remained more or less urbanely condescending. The fourth has punished my hopes by acts of self-destruction, this being the bitterest reproof. Nevertheless, I have been fortunate: four is a goodly number. A true kabbalist, and some of the hermit-masters reported on by Needham, have been granted only one disciple.

Intimacy, proximity, contemporaneity even at a distance, can feed *invidia*. the pulse beats are so difficult to diagnose because they entail currents both of love and of hatred. *Odi et amo.* These motions of spirit and sensibility reach into the undergrowths of the erotic. French exactly reflects this duality: *envie* signifies both "envy" and "desire." We admire, we revere the object of our own jealous frustration. We inflict both joy and desolation on ourselves by studying his or her works, by augmenting their celebrity, by pointing to the winner's social or material rewards. We make of ourselves the condemned shadows of these stronger lights. Our self-protective response can take two principal forms, though these may be inextricably inwoven. Adulation, discipleship are declaimed. We voice our partisan support and help disseminate the achievements of the master. In some humble, inevitably parasitic, guise we appoint ourselves agents of, participants in, his ascent and eminence. Greatness has had its "groupies" since Pythagoras, its ancillary minstrels since Homer. The adepts trooped behind their Hassidic masters shouting with secondary joy. Or we denigrate the work, most fiercely under our breath. That soiled bed may command millions on a hysterical art market, but *we* know it to be a feeble Dada joke, a late crumb off of Duchamp's table. That novel may be acclaimed as an instant classic, but *we* can demonstrate that it derives from a much finer, although forgotten forerunner. Deconstruction and post-structuralism pack the campus halls and lord it over the syllabus. *We* warm to the inward conviction that these are ephemeral fads, word games out of surrealism, which will soon recede into ridicule. Say it not in Gaza, it was not the Nobel laureate who spotted that crucial blip among radio waves. It was his assistant, unrewarded. Time will right the radiance of injustice.

A subtler, more painful mode of defensive *invidia* is that of calibrated self-abasement. Not only do we exalt the laureled; we index ourselves along axes of failure. "I am no creator. I have articulated no substantial theoretical insight. I have founded no movement or school. Broken no athletic record. Won no election. The awards I have received are of a minor or local order. I have, to borrow from Pushkin, been a courier, a *postino,* privileged to carry the mail for the poets, thinkers, political leaders, social reformers who have actually written the letters. How lucky I have been to exercise even this tributary role and walk-on part. To have been an 'attendant lord' in T. S. Eliot's famous phrase (even our abasement draws on the idiom of the great)." This self-diminution is pre-emptive. We dismiss ourselves from significance before others do so. My own placement was made irremediable when a poet, whom I had opposed and bested in public debate, having just returned from Stockholm, looked at me and said a single mocking word: "Sorry."

Such confrontations gnaw at friendship. It was not cynicism but astringent clairvoyance within a social, psychological space enfranchised by atheism, which authorized the *moralistes* to enunciate two annihilating maxims. "There is something which does not displease us in the misfortunes of a friend." And "It is not enouth to succeed, one must see others, preferably a friend, fail." Deny these nasty truths who dare. Worst is the ripening within oneself of an ironic, incorruptible recorder. Of an inner voice which derides one's illusions and articulates one's mediocrity.

Though it can test the limits of endurance, this internal witness is an indispensable tuning fork. It enforces our perception of "the real thing" every time we have (again) failed to achieve it. When a braver, more gifted contemporary has succeeded. Stifle this voice, corrupt it via *apologia* or masochistic self-pity, and truth is forfeit. Choking envy is, at the last, preferable to lying to oneself.

This complex turns purgatorial when the one concerned is seen to belong, sees himself or herself as belonging to the elite of the second rank. Cecco d'Ascoli looking on Dante. Throughout intellectual, artistic, financial, military, political, athletic enterprises and organisms, pyramids prevail. Room at the top is for the very few. Immediately below them congregate the talented, industrious, ambitious men and women of the second class. Their assemblage also need not be legion. In many intrinsic and institutional hierarchies, ranking is made publicly visible. Chinese bureaucratic examinations, as discussed in *SCC*, the French concours circus, the *summas* and *magnas* among graduands, promotion to full partnership, to the high court, to flag-rank or the first eleven, enact and publicize this taxonomy of merit. There are the elect and the almost chosen. The *Commedia* and *l'Acerba*. The actual divide may be formally or numerically trivial—a fractional point on an examination score, one hundredth of a second on the giant slalom, one black ball in the club committee or boardroom—but the gap yawns. It is non-negotiable. Genius is pitiless. In certain vocations and activities, the zones of exclusion, the barriers at the border are especially emphatic. Over and over, the impassioned amateur is crushed by the chess master who, in turn, loses to the grand master. Chess champions have been candid about the taste of triumph, about the humiliation it inflicts on the loser. There are pursuits which have the "secondary," in the full sense of the word, built into them. The functions of a discerning critic, commentator, editor are no doubt vital. They are indispensable to the dissemination and elucidation of the text. Great critics have been termed rarer than great writers.

By virtue of prose style and innovative proposals, a clutch of critics have edged into literature itself. But the fundamental fact remains: light years separate the enduring poem or fiction from the finest of critical discourse. Pushkin writes the letters. Performance is vital; it is not composition. Vice presidencies, remarked one sardonic practitioner, "are worth a bucket of hot spit."

As I have suggested, the acid of relegation bites most when a top second-rater, a *"beta plus plus"* as the Oxbridge classification shorthand graphically puts it, fully experiences the presence of the real thing. When one knows that one's own work, whatever its external rewards or seeming use, simply comes nowhere near the life force of the real thing. The frequent possibility that the work of genius will go unrecognized or be ridiculed only increases the self-lacerating ambiguity of the critic's stance. If he is honest—honesty being the only valid sanctuary for the mediocre—he will struggle to obtain hearing and justice for the first rate. He will strive for its luster however much it overshadows his own aspirations. For so many, lastingness inhabits a footnote. Can one blame the reviewer, the academic, if he or she omits saying to themselves each morning: "I write reviews of essays, books on X or Y. They never write about me"? This grim banality comports a Last Judgment.

Testimonies to this torment are unsurprisingly rare. The theme is almost taboo. It smolders between the lines of Sainte-Beuve's jealous but inspired critiques and portraits (it is, after all, an honor to be demolished by Proust). Esteemed, considered a philosophic and political prophet after the collapse of the *Reich*, Karl Jaspers is consulted with respect to Martin Heidegger's lamentable conduct under Nazism and mendacious apologias. He sets down his thoughts on his one-time friend and colleague. The *Notes on Heidegger* turn out to be a spellbinding document of unintended revelation. As he proceeds, Jaspers comes to intuit that his own acclaimed labors may fade in the light of Heidegger's outrageous, despotic stature. At his death, Max Brod, perhaps the patron saint of those who "also ran," knows that his works and days will last, for a time at least, in biographies and studies, already global, of Franz Kafka. What, then, is worse: to have been blind to genius or to have been consigned by it to the ephemeral? To have overlooked or nagged at D.'s transformative thought or to have been characterized by him as *ce petit monsieur*?

I strain every fiber to imagine that night of the 15th of September, 1327, in the cold stench of a prison cell in Florence. Can a human being breathe, relieve himself, keep from going mad or trying to commit suicide—even chained to the wall one can smash one's skull against the stones—knowing that he or she will be burned alive come morning? What expectations, what premonitions of insane pain come to possess every inch of one's consciousness as the hours both crawl and race toward dawn? Place your finger close to, or even at, the crest of a guttering candle flame. Try to rehearse, to master the incipient hurt. But between a finger and the incineration of an entire body there is no preparatory analogy. No rehearsal is possible. No pain you have ever experienced, neither gallstone nor childbirth nor the wrenching of sinews under torture can anticipate in any way that of the fire crawling up your legs, enveloping you in a blinding, suffocating hell. How long will it be before you faint? You may have heard somewhere that extinction comes more quickly if you force open your screaming mouth and breath in the smoke and fire. Will the executioner do you the infinite mercy of strangling you at the stake, of placing a small satchel of gunpowder between your roasting feet? But if there was to be that mercy, the sentence of the Holy Office would have made mention of it. No. You are to be burned *alive,* muscle by muscle, torn limb by torn limb, each hair torched, your eyes boiled out of their orbits. Consider it, picture it, fantasize what your sensations will be, all this night long. Endure the horror before the horror a thousand times over. You, Cecco d'Ascoli, prince of astrologers, physician to the Duke, familiar of the *Magna Mater,* of divine Cybele in the coolness of the Sabine hills.

Could you not have fled Florence, finding refuge among the tumultuous rivalries of local potentates and bishops? Or made peace with the Inquisitor? Have you misread your own horoscope and failed to see the abyss which lay in waiting? Or did Cecco, during that night of terror, allow the possibility that the stars and planetary conjunctions could lie? That they could, by some hideous malice, deceive their acolyte? Perhaps the astral powers had grown jealous of one who read them too clearly. Prophecy, the necromantic unriddling of the future were considered impious. So affirms Book X of the *Inferno.* It may have seemed as if a further blackness, at once void and mocking, had seeped into his cell. And now it was not starlight nor the flicker of the Zodiac he looked to, but the first streaks of his last morning.

Not only his living flesh would be burned. All his writings were to be tossed on to the pyre. So far as d'Ascoli could foresee, nothing of his mountainous labors, all in manuscript, would survive. All would be made ash. The incomplete *l'Acerba,* his epic masterpiece, would vanish without trace. Whereas Dante's *Commedia* was on its assured road to immortality. Whereas Dante's Tuscan was already silencing its linguistic competitors. It has all been in vain, says a voice out of the pit of horror. In a moment of ultimate clairvoyance and concentration, Cecco knows that he has been the more or less scorned contemporary, invidious rival to Dante's supreme genius and fame. Conceivably the anguish which this realization brought was, momentarily at least, even crueller than the apprehension of imminent, unspeakably agonizing death.

Given the context of the Institute in Princeton, the house of Einstein and of Gödel, and then that of Harvard and of Cambridge

University, I have been privileged to observe "the real thing." Twice, I have heard the phone call from Stockholm ring in the office next door. And been invited to join in that evening's celebrations. I have brushed against major poets and novelists, interviewed masters of theory, of anthropology, of social thought who have stamped our age, some of whose names have become adjectives in many languages. My luck has been extraordinary. A teacher, a critic, a commentator or publicist can open doors for the creators. He can quicken to deserved life what has been censored or overlooked. It is a blessed condition. It is, nonetheless, strictly secondary and auxiliary. A-minus at very best. A line by René Char haunts me: *"N'est pas minuit qui veut."* ("Is not midnight who wishes to be so," where *minuit* can stand for poetic or intellectual revelation, where it can be another name for Paul Celan or Char himself, or Francis Crick.) Very soon, if one is lucid, the future lies behind one. In transparent defensiveness, one might entitle one's autobiography *Errata*.

I did not write the study of Cecco d'Ascoli. It might have been of some interest. But it came too near the bone.

THE TONGUES OF EROS

WHAT IS THE SEXUAL life of a deaf-mute? To what incitements and cadence does he or she masturbate? How does the deaf-mute experience libido and consummation? It would be extremely difficult to obtain reliable evidence. I am not aware of any body of systematic inquiry. Yet the question is of acute significance. It addresses the nerve centers of the interrelations between eros and language. It brings into baffled focus the absolutely decisive issue of the semantic structure of sexuality, of its linguistic dynamics. Sex is spoken and listened to, aloud or in silence, externally or internally, before, during, and after intercourse. The two communicative currents, the two enactments are indissoluble. Ejaculation is integral to both. The rhetoric of desire is a category of discourse in which the neurophysiological generation of speech acts and that of lovemaking engage reciprocally. Punctuation is analogous: the male orgasm is an exclamation mark. What is known of the sexuality of the blind demonstrates the cardinal functions of internalized representation, of a verbalized imagery in which linguistic and tactile values inform and reinforce each other. At no other interface in the human fabric are neurochemical components and what we take to be the circuits of consciousness and subconsciousness so intimately fused. Here mentality and the organic compose a unified synapse. Neurology ascribes sexual reflexes to the parasympathetic nervous system. Psychology adduces voluntary impulses and responses when analyzing human sexual proceedings. The concept of "instinct," itself only dimly understood, characterizes the crucial zone of interaction between the carnal and the cerebral, between genitalia and spirit. This zone is saturated with language.

The elements of this linguistic immersion—we move in and out of speech when preparing, having, and recalling sex—are so numerous and intricate, the narrative is under such pressures of feeling, as to defy any comprehensive listing, let alone agreed-upon classification. Speech is held to be both universal and private, collective and individual. Every unimpeded woman or man draws, automatically as it were, on the pre-existent, available store-house of words and grammatical constructs. We move within the diction-ary and grammar of possibility. Proportionately to our mental ca-pacities, social milieu, schooling, location, and historical inheritance, we construe our idiom. But even when steeped in the same collective ethos and ethnic, economic and social environ-ment, each and every human being, ranging from the moronic and scarcely articulate to the verbally endowed, develops a more or less efficient "idiolect," this is to say a code of lexical and syntactic means singular to themselves. Nicknames, phonetic associations, covert references signal such singularities. Where it does not pur-pose tautology, as in formal and symbolic logic, language, even rudimentary, is polysemous, many-layered, expressive of inten-tionalities only imperfectly revealed or articulated. It encodes. This encoding can indeed be perceptible, arising out of shared memories, historical aspirations, political and social contexts. But it can also conceal essential, individualized, intensely privatized needs and significations. Language is in and of itself multilingual. It contains worlds. Just consider the language of children. More often than not, articulate enunciation is the iceberg tip of sub-merged, implicit meanings. We speak, we hear "between the lines." Understanding, reception are acts of attempted decipherment, of code breaking.

Nowhere is this "interlinearity" more pervasive, more forma-tive than in the echo chambers of the erotic. It is a commonplace that the rhetoric and verbal stage-management of seduction is replete with half-truths, with borrowed clichés or outright falsehoods, which, in turn, have to be glossed by the object of desire. The sounds which accompany orgasm, often poised at the threshold of verbalization, sometimes seeming to echo back to the prehistory of language, can be deliberately mendacious. They have their brute poetics of hypocrisy just as do the flourishes and dramatized sincerities of erotic eloquence. Monologue and dialogue—or more precisely monologue in tandem—can alternate, can meld in a wealth of cadence and nuance virtually impossible to analyze systematically. One intuits that during masturbation word and image are more tightly connected, more "dialectically" energized than in any other human communicative process. Joyce's letters to Nora bear pulsing witness to this interaction. Even by itself, a word, a sound cluster can trigger breathless arousal (the celebrated *faire catleya* in Proust). The image deploys itself within the sound. Thus masturbation has its mute grammar. Within its privacies, however, in the recesses of the intimate, public agencies are at work. The erotic and sexual phraseology of the media, the amorous jargon of film and television, the tidal declamation of advertisement and the mass market, stylize, conventionalize the rhythm, the pace, the discursive components of millions of partners. In the developed world, with its corrosive pornography, countless lovers, particularly among the young, "program" their lovemaking, whether consciously or not, along prepackaged semiotic lines. What should be the most spontaneously anarchic, individually exploratory and inventive of human encounters, is to a very large degree *scripted*. The last freedom, the final authenticity may indeed be that of the deaf-mute. We do not know.

I have argued in *After Babel* (1975) that the thousandfold multiplicity of mutually incomprehensible languages once spoken on this

Earth—so many are now extinct or disappearing—is not, as mythologies and allegories of disaster would have it, a curse. It is, on the contrary, a blessing and a jubilation. Each and every human tongue is a window on being, on creation. A window like no other. There are no "small" languages however reduced their demographic or environmental setting. Certain languages spoken in the Kalahari Desert feature more and subtler ramifications of the subjunctive than were available to Aristotle. Hopi grammars possess nuances of temporality and motion more consonant with the physics of relativity and undecidability than are our own Indo-European and Anglo-Saxon resources. By virtue of the cultural-psychological roots and development embedded within them, roots which also in the etymological sense reach back into the subconscious, every tongue voices identity and experience in its own irreducibly particular way. It segments time in manifold and diverse units. Numerous grammars do not formally divide tenses into past, present, and future. The "stasis" of Hebrew verb forms entails a metaphysics and, indeed, a theological model of history. There are languages in the Andes, for example, in which, most reasonably, the future lies behind the speaker, being invisible, whereas the horizons of the past lie open to view before him (there are intriguing analogies here with Heidegger's ontology). Space, which is a social no less than a neurophysiological construct, is linguistically mapped and inflected. Languages inhabit it differently. Via their "cartography" and nominations, the relevant linguistic communities underline or efface varying contours and features. The spectrum of precise discrimination between various tints and textures of snow in Eskimo languages, the color charts which differentiate the pelts of horses in the jargon of the Argentine *gaucho,* are standard examples. The axes of the human body whereby we orient ourselves in our local spaces are linguistically labeled and realized. British dialects produce more than one hundred words and phrases for left-handedness. The equation between left-handedness and evil (*sinistra*) is enshrined in Mediterranean cultures. Structural anthropology has taught us that concepts and identifications of kinship are ineluctably linguistic. Even such basic notions as parenthood or incest depend on taxonomies, on lexical and grammatical encoding inseparable from the options— collective, economic, historical, ritual—set out in speech. We verbalize, we "phrase," as does music, our relations to ourselves and to others. "I" and "thou" are facts of syntax. There are linguistic vestiges in which this distinction is blurred, for example in the archaic Greek dual. Though it may take on "surrealist" modes, the grammatology of our dreams is linguistically organized and diversified far beyond the historically, socially circumscribed provincialities of the psychoanalytic. How enriching it might be to have nightmares or wet dreams in, say, Albanian.

The consequence is a boundless wealth of possibility. Every human tongue challenges reality in its own unique manner. There are as many constellations of futurity, of hope, of religious, metaphysical, and political projection, "dreaming forward," as there are optative and counterfactual verb forms. Hope is empowered by syntax. I have conjectured, without being able to offer proof, that the generative justification for the "crazy" number and fragmentation of tongues—more than four hundred in India alone—is analogous to the Darwinian model of adaptive niches. Every language exploits and transmits different aspects, different potentialities of the human circumstance. Every language has its own strategies of negation and imagining. These enable it to say "No" to the physical, material constraints on our existence. Owing to language(s), we can defy or attenuate the monochrome of predestined mortality. Each negation has its own stubborn transcendence. It is this scandal of inextinguishable "hope against hope" which enables us to endure, to recover from the perennial murderousness and absurdity of our material and historical condition. It is the seemingly wasteful plethora of languages which allows us to articulate alternatives to reality, to speak freedom within servitude, to program plenty within destitution. Without the great octave of possible grammars such negation and "alterity," this wager on tomorrow would not be feasible.

Hence the truly irreparable loss, the diminution in the chances of man, when a language dies. With such a death, it is not only a vital lineage of remembrance—past tenses or their equivalent—it is not only a landscape, realistic or mythical, a calendar that is blotted out: it is configurations of a conceivable future. A window closes on zero. The extinction of languages which we are now witnessing—dozens pass annually into irretrievable silence—is precisely parallel to the ravaging of fauna and flora, but with greater finality. Trees can be replanted, the DNA of animal species can, in part at least, be conserved and perhaps reactivated. A dead language stays dead or survives as a pedagogic relic in the academic zoo. The consequence is a drastic improverishment in the ecology of the human psyche. The true catastrophe at Babel is not the scattering of tongues. It is the reduction of human speech to a handful of planetary, "multinational" tongues. This reduction, formidably fuelled by the mass market and information technology, is now reshaping the globe. Military-technocratic megalomania, the imperatives of commercial greed, are making of Anglo-American standardized vocabularies and grammars an Esperanto. Due to its inherent difficulty, Chinese may not usurp this sad sovereignty. When India does, its language will be some variant of Anglo-American. Thus there was a nauseating but uncanny simulacrum of the mystery at Babel in the collapse of the twin World Trade Center towers on the eleventh of September.

The blessing of creative variousness obtains not only as between different languages, this is to say "interlingually." It is richly operative within any given tongue, intralingually. The most compendious of dictionaries is no more than an abridged shorthand, obsolete even as it is published. Lexical and grammatical usage inside any spoken or written tongue is in perpetual motion and fission. It hives off into local and regional dialects. The agencies of differentiation are at work as between social classes, explicit or submerged ideologies, faiths, professions. Parlance can vary from urban district to district, from hamlet to hamlet. In ways only partly elucidated, speech is molded by gender. Women and men often do not purpose or signify the same thing when uttering or writing the identical word. Not taking "No" for an answer is a symbolic pointer. Shifts in meaning and intentionality within and across generations are constant. At certain moments in social history, in familial awareness, in the reflexes of mutual recognition, these shifts can turn dramatic. This looks to be so in our accelerated present, between age groups separated by the very mechanics of information. Thus different levels in society, different localities, genders, age groups can come close to mutual incomprehension. The fountain pen does not speak to the iPod.

Linguistic fragmentation serves both aggressive and defensive needs. We speak "for" ourselves and in solicitation, subversion or defiance of the other. Even the most urbane, grammatically schooled of utterances will contain particles of "slang" calculated to accentuate intimacy or exclusion. The elite school boy, the freshman, the greenhorn cadet are made to memorize these nuances when joining their peers. The jargon of the street gang, of the soccer hooligan is no less snobbish, no less ritualized. It follows that each and every semantic exchange, be it in the same language and even among intimates—perhaps most sharply there—comports a more or less conscious, a more or less labored, process of translation. There is no message, no arc of communication between source and reception, which does not have to be decoded. Immediacy of understanding is an idealization of silence. Customarily, decoding occurs on the instant and, as it were, unnoticed. But when tensions, private or public, arise, when distrust or irony or some element of falsehood hum their background noise, reciprocal interpretation, the hermeneutic act, can become arduous and uncertain. Auxiliary signals come into play. Pitch, inflection, intonation, body language can both clarify and conceal. It is the unspoken which is loudest.

In the languages of eros and of sex, these attributes and opacities are brought to their highest degree of intricate intensity. As I have suggested, there is no other realm of human conduct in which physiology presses as fiercely on mentality (itself a problematic, contested demarcation). During sex, the subconscious drums its way into every fiber of nervous impulse and sensibility. Imagination is made flesh, it—in Shakespeare's consummate phrasing—"bodies forth." In turn, flesh imagines and cries out. Here is incarnation if ever there be. The etymological accord is factitious, but "semen" and "semantic" are conjoined in ejaculations both corporeal and linguistic. I have already alluded to the "private parts" of speech. These activate both monologue and dialogue. The language current in onanism as well as that in shared intercourse, itself a term of communication, alternates between diachronic and social counters on the one hand and personal, covert, singular reference on the other. It is here that "private languages" flourish. The most shopworn, flatly colloquial turn can take on a wealth of secret provocation, of hermetic incitement. Masturbation enacts the paradoxes of soliloquy. Inaudibly or out loud, the verbal stream implodes voices, sounds, metaphors, memories, and anticipations. We overhear ourselves in a complicated process of auditory voyeurism. In the case of the sub-literate, this compaction is presumably somewhat threadbare and repetitive. The richer our lexical, grammatical inventory, the more inventive our inward orchestration. I refer again to the corruscating virtuosities of erotic self-address in Joyce's letters and *Ulysses*; but John Cowper Powys, "a furiously inspired masturbator," is hardly less en-

dowed. When two or more parties are at play—mutual masturbation is a perennial theme in erotica and pornography—the variants
are too nuanced and numerous to list (though Sade attempts precisely this exhaustive indexing in an obsessive parody of Enlightenment encyclopedias). Couples contrive their particular dialects
of desire and release. Their bedroom idiom is more often than not
derived from public sources, from print and the graphic media. But
given imaginative resources, it can assume esoteric, neological,
wholly private modes. Updike's novels have an acute ear for these
compulsive privacies and inventions of sexual exchange. Lovers
bestow on each other gifts of hidden signification. They name the
objects, the circumstances which furnish their erotic spaces in an
Adamic motion of re-creation. They literally entitle parts of their
bodies, sexual postures, the intimacies which precede nakedness.
Nabokov celebrates these pulsating donations, particularly between partners whose native tongues differ (I will come back to
this). The lover will bid the beloved speak these words, com-
pounding excitement. There is a dizzying narration of this ritual in
an Edna O'Brien fiction. Where sexual congress, an archaic but
telling designation, becomes what physics calls the uresolved
"three-body problem," the confluence of private and public discourse, of commonplace and novelty, can grow almost indecipherable. There are stages in the inwoven, polysemic lexicon and
syntax of Shakespeare's sonnets when a third voice seems to in-
trude upon, to enrich, but also to deconstruct that of the couple.
This game is made the more polyphonic by the notorious masking
or ambiguities of gender. We watch the *pas de deux* and *de trois* of
such word clusters as "spend," "expend," and "expense" across the
fabric of the verse.

In consequence, every language and subset within that language energizes, narrates, recalls sex in its own specific key. This
proceeding is in perpetual motion; it changes constantly. There are
even distinct numerologies of eros. Consider the meaning of "69"

in modern Western allusion. These variables inform every component in lovemaking and sexual verbalization, be it private or public, solitary or combinatorial. Seduction, foreplay, coitus, the afterword to orgasm, the subsequent narrative, internalized or voiced, differ as much as do vocabularies and grammars themselves. Every tongue and stratum within that tongue will draw different boundaries between proper and taboo expressions, between night words and licit usages. It will in subtle but imperative ways segment, cadence the pace and rhythm of lovemaking, the chronometer of masturbatory or conjoined arousal and release. Different languages and languages within languages deliniate, symbolize, evaluate erotically different bodily parts and functions in their own perspective. They name or disguise them accordingly. Renaissance poetry details the human sexual physique; it dwells on *les blasons du corps*. What is a licensed designation and nakedness in one system of speech acts is hidden, even sacramental, in others. At the ardent center of this labyrinth lie the performative associations between semantic orality and the manifold practices of oral sex. "Tongues" are of the essence in both the discursive and the physiological repertoire. Lips are instrumental to both. The epigrams of Martial are a guide to this hybrid crux. Discretely veiled, cross-references between eloquence and fellation or cunnilingus glow in the undertones of baroque and libertine verse.

There exist a fair number of monographs on sexual terms, lexica of the erotic, glossaries of the pornographic. These customarily crop up under the rubric of ethnographic curiosa. The bawdy of individual writers such as Rabelais and Shakespeare has been analyzed. There are studies of sexual innuendo and double entendre in Restoration comedy and the partly clandestine fiction of the Enlightenment (in Rochester, for example, in Crébillon and Diderot). The jargons, the slang of prostitution, ranging from classical antiquity to the Edwardian, has been catalogued. As have been various registers of sexual diction amid different ethnic groups and the criminal underworld. There is guidance to the rich sexual connotations of the lyrics of Afro-American jazz (itself a sex word), hip-hop and heavy metal. Somewhere, no doubt, someone is searching for secret erotic undertones in Jane Austen. Legal theory and judicial practice have wrestled, largely in vain, with the dilemma of verbal and pictorial obscenity. The problem is intractable because the relevant demarcations are always mobile and ideologically fuelled classifications. Judicial approaches to pornography and its means of expression constitute a genre of their own, largely indecisive. (What comes closer to obscenity than certain passages in *Cymbeline?*) The tsunami of the pornographic in our mass media, the constantly mutating role of sex speech among the young and the disheveled have become an object of unnerved attention, itself often prurient. Perhaps permissiveness is the only common sense.

What is lacking is any methodical, historically and psychologically responsible phenomenology of the interplay between sexuality and words, between libido and enunciation, either internalized or vocal. We have no systematic poetic or rhetoric of eros, of how the making of love is a making of words and syntax. No Aristotle, no Saussure has taken up this pivotal challenge. More specifically, we have, so far as I am aware, no study, even summary, of how sex is experienced, of how love is made in different languages and different language-sets (ethnic, economic, social, local). Per se, the polyglot condition at varying levels of immediacy and proficiency is not all that rare. It features in numerous communities, such as Sweden, Switzerland, Malaysia. A multitude of men and women dispose of more than one "native" tongue, from very earliest childhood. Yet we seem to have no valid account, no introspective or socialized record of what must be their metamorphic erotic lives. how does lovemaking in Basque or Russian differ from that in Flemish or Korean? What privileges or inhibitions arise between lovers with different first languages? Is *coitus* also, perhaps fundamentally, translation? No polyglot woman or man, so far as I know, has left a record of her and his sexuality within and between languages. Although theoretically it can be, actual love is rarely made in either silence or Esperanto.

I have every reason to believe that there is a "Don Juanism" of the polyglot, an eros of the multilingual. I believe that an individual man or woman fluent in several tongues seduces, possesses, remembers differently according to his or her use of the relevant language. That the love and lechery of the polyglot differs from that of the monoglot, faithful to one language, as the suggestive phrase has it. My words "wound you," says Shakespeare's Alcibiades in *Timon of Athens*. In eros this ache will differ from language to language, from dialect to dialect. Don Juan himself is reputed to exhibit his amorous wares and triumphs in Spanish, Italian, French, German, Russian and a host of other tongues. He glides between the conventions of aristocratic address, of philosophic irony and the semi-literate speech of the peasantry. But he has left us no report of this "infinite variety." Is there any document we can look to?

Giacomo Casanova's memoirs are famously unreliable. No matter. Their psychological acumen, the bravura and candor of their social notations remain invaluable. Two axioms are paramount: "Without words the pleasure of love is lessened by at least two thirds"; and "My mind and my material part are one and the same substance." Language is fused with sex not only for strategic or mundane motives. The speaking of eros and the play of sex are in unison within organic life itself. The Chevalier de Seingalt is an inspired polygot (he contemns Jews but was himself, very probably, of Jewish provenance). The twelve-volume *chronique scandaleuse* of his actual and fabled exploits is a Berlitz guide to lust. Casanova discriminates between the poetic merits, the musicalities, the fashionable resouces of numerous forms of Italian. Venetian is itself multiple, taking in not only the patrician and populist language of the *Serenissima,* but the dialects, almost autochthonous, of the adjacent communities in the Lagoon (Goldoni's comedies bear witness to their lexical and grammatical strengths). Casanova points to the diverse characteristics of Paduan, Milanese, Bolognese, Tuscan branches of Italian. He considers the vaunted purities of Sienese speech and the many-layered energies of Neapolitan. If his ease in Latin seems considerable, so does his command of Roman and ecclesiastical rhetoric. He aspires to only "little Spanish." At one point, he cites the Hebrew Bible in its original. Though London, Amsterdam, and St. Petersburg are very much part of Casanova's atlas, it is via the universality of French that he makes himself heard and understood in these borderlands. Dutch and Turkish do seem to elude him. But there are hints at rudiments of Portuguese.

Every scenario of "speech-sex," if one can put it that way, figures in Casanova's adventures. Seduction is smoothed by the discovery of a shared language. Or impeded, both farcically and gravely, by mutual incomprehension. The lady speaks only English or Polish. German is available, but Swiss-German turns out to be as "Genoese is to Italian." By moonlight, accent or inaccuracies of idiom can betray: the veiled nun is not Venetian, but French. Erotic signals can depend on nuance: "In polite Neapolitan, the first token of friendship which a gentleman or a lady bestows on a new acquaintance is to use the second person singular in addressing him." Complicity blossoms. But elsewhere, linguistic misunderstandings and flawed translations impede amorous bliss. There are as many shadings of Parmesan as there are local cheeses. How is he to know that *décharger* is an inadmissible vulgarity when uttered in a lady's presence, though she be in bed? Where La Charpillon keeps her admirable legs closed, Casanova's inflamed libido explodes into "every possible" semantic key: "gentlesness, anger, reasonableness, remonstration, threats, rage, despair, prayers, tears, vilifications, atrocious insults." The strumpet wields a supreme weapon: "She resisted me for three whole hours without ever answering." For Casanova, silence equals erotic defeat or impotence. As old age and bodily infirmity loom, language becomes sex. Orgasm modulates into the climax of narrative, of remembered felicities. Casanova's recollections attain a Proustian finesse: "We looked at each other without speaking, we spoke to each other not knowing what we were saying." Caresses no longer carry their promise of immortality. The Chevalier leaves his lover to return to Dover. The other ten or twelve passengers are seasick: "I was only sad." *Post coitum.*

In German, the verb can be, most often is placed at the close of a sentence, however serpentine, however intricately suspended. Meaning holds its pent-up breath before dynamic, terminal release. An analogy with intercourse suggests itself. "Interruption" and orgasmic fulfillment. It is an analogy only, an allegory of syntax. Yet it may throw some light into the psychic and neurological deeps where linguistic structures both incite and discharge sexuality.

When undressing, S. almost unthinkingly mouthed and hummed a children's rhyme. In which castration—the butcher's knife in pursuit of sausage-stealing urchins—was clearly audible. A warning to me, a hint of contempt for my visible desire? German nursery rhymes and juvenilia are crowded with masturbatory, coital, scatological encoding and allusion. In German, somewhat more than in other languages I know (or is this an unjust impression?), the primordial interplay of sex and sadism, of intercourse and aggression, of orgasm and pain, of the infantile and the adult, runs like a taunting thread through the ditties and comical ballads familiar to children from an early age. Wilhelm Busch's *Max und Moritz* is often terrifying, and that terror, made playfully macabre, resounds in the hobbyhorse refrain of the orphaned child at the homicidal close to Alban Berg's *Wozzeck*. S. pouted, there is no better word, as she stepped out of her underwear. But her humming sometimes ended on the mocking trill of a bird. As are other Indo--European glossaries, German is prodigal in its identification of male sexual penetration with the pecking of birds (English "pecker," French *becqueter*). In German, this equation goes further. Sexual ingress is quite literally "birding." German seems to occupy a pivotal chord in that gamut of *f* sounds which arches from Latinate "fornication" to French *foutre*, Italian *fottare*, English *fucking*. (What is it about that *f* ?) German *vögeln* is full of beaks and claws. No one imaged that onrush of libidinal terror more incisively than Hitchcock. Natural functions play a persistent role in German eros. The excitement, the merriment they provide is regressively infantile, thus preserving a touch of innocence. S., but also Ch., commanded a graphic, wide-ranging vocabulary for the ambiguous felicities—ambiguous because replete with disciplinary and transgressive reminiscences—of urinating and defecating. Urinating together, "lest we make in our pants," clearly a childhood fear and prohibition, became a ritual of complicity and arousal. This sharing did not extend to defecation. S. was wonderfully awake to Yeats's finding that love dwells in the house of excrement, but regarded any witness to her shitting as utterly perverse. I have heard Ch. whispering a couplet in which bird droppings were compared to her own. Thus in the utterances of sex in German: wings beat, claws grip, beaks hammer with especial and graphic vehemence. Like so many allegorists and anatomists of eros, Ch. regarded her pubic hair as a "nest." Do we not, she rightly asked, speak of women's "eggs" (this, quite loudly, at breakfast, in one of Munich's more decorous hotels)?

Beneath Ch.'s sanitized, academic German persisted the baroque lilt of her Bavarian origins. When nearing climax, she would cry out, though in a muted register, the name "*Sankt* Nepomuk the

Lesser." A dim personage in the church calendar, this early medieval sanctified soul had his shrine in a lost corner near the Tyrolean border. Carved in limewood, the saint brandished a memorably elongated index finger. Invoking him, in either thanks or propitiation, Ch. called up memories of fantastications centered on that appendage. These had been shared during onanism with a coven of friends in her convent-school dormitory. Fervently imagined and mimed, *Sankt* Nepomuk's finger pointed the way to solitary yet also communal bliss. It would be rewarding to inquire into the differences in sexual slang, in the sex lingo of adolescence between Roman Catholic and Lutheran regions of Germany. Ch. proudly maintained that her resources comprised no less than a dozen censored designations for the vagina of pubescent girls, with a lexical subsection specific to the presumed virginity and "itches" suffered by nuns and postulants. She referred to this cascade of taboo words as her "rosary." Inevitably, a number of these sobriquets referred to candles (the well-known parody of a line in *Macbeth* plays on this association). Had Lutheran sobriety any comparable riches?

V.'s grammar of lovemaking was that of Viennese. She mapped her own opulent physique and that of her lover(s) with place-names derived from the capital's varied districts and suburbs. Thus "taking the street-car to Grinzing" signified a gentle, somewhat respectful anal access. Sipping the light, golden new wine in one of the suburban cafés on the way to the Semmering referred to her readiness, only very occasionally granted, to imbibe her partner's urine. "Give me a sip of *Heuriger*"—spoken sotto voce; the remembrance of that invitation still makes me dizzy. Highly perceptive, V. intuited that the theories and explanations offered by that "bizarre" Jewish sex doctor Freud, in fact hinged on the peculiarities of Viennese parlance in the moneyed, feminized bourgeoisie of his time (so largely Jewish). Freud's dream decipherments and chains of verbal association were founded on a specialized, ephemeral linguistic corpus. Even those phallic cigars and sharply pointed umbrellas told of "a local habitation and a name." *Herr* Freud, opined V., knew nothing of the night talk and scatological laughter of the common herd. Her own dreams were brimful of cats, chamber pots and left-handed firemen. What had Freud to say to that?

The underground volume of sex slang and bawdy in German is no doubt as extensive as it is in other tongues. Yet it seems to lack a certain verve and oblique poetry. Strikingly, German literature has rarely matched the classics of European *libertinage*. Where is its *Fanny Hill* or, in modern terms, its *Histoire d'O*? German only seldom generates that middle ground between abstraction and grossness, between sublimity and warming filth. I do not recall the name of the lady, only the lashing rain which drove us to a nearby hotel. And the torsions, both awkward and choreographic, whereby she wound out of her sodden tights. She insisted that neither the setting nor the situation were habitual to her (whether or not this was in fact so). "Am I myself? Are you?" The question, unknowingly to be sure, seemed to stem directly out of Fichte's meditations on the cancellation of the self. To make love in German can be taxing.

Clichés, but on target: musicality, a sensual timbre like no other, an inherent inflection toward masculine prepotence, an easy flowering toward hyperbole, an organic impulse to prolixity and the oratorical, a delicate yet also vividly carnal shaping of the lips for the appropriate vowels—all these do characterize Italian. But there is, of course, no single, canonic "Italian." The languages remain a mosaic of regional, local usages, shading from idiomatic nuances and dialect to near autonomy. Bergamo has its own lexicon and grammar. Neapolitan and Sicilian forms are virtually closed to the outsider. The dictionary of desire in Lucca is not that in use in Bari. We saw all this with reference to Casanova. In no other European tongue, moreover, is linguistic history and development as intimately wired into the history of love. *La nuova lingua e il nuovo eros* are indissociable. The vulgate discovers, asserts its own auroral means in love poetry. This revelation informs Dante's *Vita Nuova*. Out of its distant roots in Ovid, in Propertius, in French and Sicilian romance, but also in Oriental texts, the *amor cortese* of the eighteenth century cultivates a polyphonic code, allowing modulations from adoration of the most sublimated order to ardent lust, from untainted light to flame. Integral to Italian discourses of love, as they unfold in Dante's predecessors, in Dante himself, in Petrarch and Boccaccio, is a determinant Catholic ambivalence as to guilt and sensuality, as to the corporeal and the transcendent. This uneasy symbiosis is eloquent in the rich statements of homoerotic or frankly homosexual relations from Michelangelo's Neo-Platonic amities to Pasolini's debauche. This lineage enlists a certain misogyny unmistakable even in heterosexual contexts. Its articulate expression is ferocious in Moravia. Women are held responsible for men's *bestiale appetito*. They can be labeled a *sospetoso animale* in the Decameron. Yet an Italian woman is imperatively a "mother" in the palpable image of the "Mother of God." From this ambivalence and tension, old age and the twilight of impotence are a bleak release. Svevo records this humiliating liberation in his *Senilità*.

A Neapolitan colleague, an ethnolinguist, introduced me to the labyrinthine underworld of local sexual speech. He listed some nineteen appellations for the male organ, two of them derived from Arabic, one, possibly, from vestiges of Byzantine Greek. The linguistic range for testicles, which can be touched quite publicly in invocation of good luck, is no less prodigal. Charged, they can be hailed in heroic, almost chivalric terms. Aged and withered, they are subject to mockery. This range plays both humorously and warily, as in other European languages, on the crossovers between "balls and "purses," between sperm and coin. The dialectic of male potency and wealth or destitution is intuited precisely throughout Ben Jonson's *Volpone* and Iago's advice to Roderigo to "put money in his purse" in Shakespeare's *Othello*. In English, "to spend" retains this duality. Unlike German, Italian colloquialism avoids abstractions where concreteness and the images which it fosters will do. The excremental—the variousness of body fluids, together with deeply entrenched superstitions—displays its elemental truths in the argot and idiom of sex. A robust veracity, but touched upon by intimations of the uncanny, of the demonic, particularly in rural, southern Italy, energizes a wealth of proverbs, of talismanic saying, of "speech gestures." Ethnographers at work in the more isolated regions of the Abruzzi and Calabria have recorded an array of proverbs which pivot on the blurred lines between human and animal intercourse. Of these, a handful reflect actual bestiality as it may arise from the needs and solitudes of the goatherd. At its populist levels, Italian sexual sayings are immersed in the honesties of the body, animal and human, whereas Italian lyric-philosophic celebrations of love attain matchless spirituality and neo-Platonic transfiguration. Thus the pilgrimage of love in the *Commedia* is also an ascent from the obscentities of the infernal ("there is Paradise in that Hell," noted Sade) to the failures of all language on the ecstatic threshold of the angelic.

It was in Genoa that A.-M. instructed me in the litany of seduction. I suspect that verbal foreplay, generated in part by social convention, in part by aroused spontaneity, is so significant in Italian because it enacts the more or less hypocritical homage of masculine lust to feminine recalcitrance. Of these preliminaries Mozart's Don Giovanni is past master. Scholars have it that the "language of flowers," the encryption of loving hopes and motions in the names and guise of flowers, may hark back to ancient Persian. Horticulture was A.-M.'s other passion. She was a virtuoso of floral innuendos and shorthand. The game began over coffee. Not the rushed espresso downed by millions of Italians on their way to work, but the afternoon or early evening brew sipped by lovers at the shadowy back of the bar. The catalogue of Italian coffees is extensive. Every nuance of strength, of sweetness, of latte, cream, cinnamon, grated chocolate figures. (Why is there so potent an erotic suggestion in cappuccino? Why so evident a hint of loneliness, of parting, in a *ristretto*?) Then came the flowers.

A.-M. took pride in the thicket of her "burning bush." Gardens are the scene of assignation, of sexual witchcraft (as in Tasso). First my tongue was to brush, barely brush, the dew from the outer petals. Penetration could ensue only with almost unbearable *rallentando* and lightness. The violets must be woken from their dusky sleep, the marigolds plucked leaf by vibrant leaf, the lobelias gently watered with saliva. Only then might one proceed to the inner grotto, now scented and alive with wetness as is a fountain hidden by moss (cf. Petrarch). A recess in which, as in virtually all heraldry of eros, bloomed the dark rose of ecstasy, magically unfolding. A.-M. may not have come across Ariel, but knew that "Where the bee sucks, there sucks I." And brushed my lips with what she called "her honey." Or the nacreous spoor of the snail, housed in the recesses of the arbour. "My bee," she whispered "is your sac now full?" One (probably unmentionable) caresse was referred to as "our flowering cactus."

At the opposite extreme, we find the sadistic economy of the proletarian adolescents, of the hoodlums and rent boys in Pasolini's reportage. The serial oral sex in *Petrolio* makes language gag. Set the savage minimalism of Pasolini next to the mauve *cantabile* of D'Annunzio's amorous rhetoric. Both are shot through with either the presence or that afterglow of Catholic rites and imaginings. Expressive of a valuation of erotic desire and consummation, of sin and sanctification—fellatio as communion—Italian dwells on the immense cliché of love's affinity to death. Millennially before Freud it proclaims the hunger of the male for his mother. More ancient, even, more numinous than any Christian subsoil, are the pagan remnants which surface in countless folk-tales, ceremonies and talismanic gestures. In the Romagna, couples still copulate, or did so into the twentieth century, leaning against a stone thought to be a pagan altar or the phallus of a lost god. "Now let *me* drink," said A.-M. In that quartet of languages which speak my identity, Italian is the viola or *viola d'amore,* arching from deepest mahogany to spun gold.

To make love in Italian is to know that certain days run to twenty-five hours.

Folk wisdom, trashy but ubiquitous, ascribes to French culture and sensibility a specific, often blatant amorousness. The exaltation of *l'amour,* of sexual pursuits—the chase and the quarry—is held to characterize multiple facets of French life, from perfume and lingerie to art and entertainment, from the streets of Pigalle to the deer gardens of Versailles, from the smooching of the crooners to the licentious indiscretions of politicians. Widespread among Anglo-Saxons has been the conviction that sexual initiation and erotic transgression are best sought in France. The opening chime of Sterne's *Sentimental Journey* celebrates this assumption. Even an observer as discriminating as Henry James regarded French psychology and fiction as sexually obsessed and took Paris to be the capital of "living," when that verb is charged with erotic implications. The wet dreams of generations of English and American adolescents have led to the Seine.

In fact, however, Gallic civilization is, in many respects, constrained and puritanical. It is no more licentious than any other. If anywhere, Babylon in its modern guise has been identified with Amsterdam, Copenhagen, San Francisco or Bangkok. Extensive domains of French public and private life, notably in the provinces, in *la France profonde,* have been *bourgeois* to a degree. As in other cultures, this conservatism is attended by hypocrisy, by an intricate concoction of cant and consensual cover-up: the local ecstasies, the brothel lurk out of sight behind lace curtains. Simenon bears authoritative witness to the requisite tactics of discretion. But there is simply no evidence that the French libido is, of itself, more ardent or adventurous than that of any other developed society or that French men and women expend more time and energy on sexual encounters than do their neighbors in other nations. The flamboyant mythologies are those of tourism and commercial exploitation.

Indeed, the first element, the opening gambits which strike one in French erotic exchanges is their *formality*. This can be awesome. Gloriously astride me, my first teacher in the arts of orgasm, praise God, an older woman burnished by irony and compassion, bade me "come, come now and deep." But did so using the formal *vous*. French couples have, in the midst of coitus, done so for centuries. Resort to familiar *tu* can, when not explicitly granted, lead, as I discovered to my cost, to fuming rebuke. "How dare you address me as *tu*?" panted V. even as I parted her comely legs: *comment osez-vous*? Matters are now changing under pressure of the media and the cult of vulgarity. As I came of age, and in affairs during my younger years, subjunctives would turn up at truly unexpected moments. On one occasion, in a hotel in Angers, a subjunctive pluperfect—Proust may have been among the last to handle these with ease—arrested me in, as it were, mid-flow. Ceremonies of syntax attend on French intercourse.

In consequence, the prodigal utterances and invocations of the libidinous in French literature, and this includes its wealth of pornography, tend to rely on a formulaic semantic storage. From the *Roman de la rose* to Sagan, from Villon to *Madame Bovary* and Apollinaire, the idiom, the dialects of desire incline to be stylized and fundamentally economic. The summits of sexual possession, of possessing and being possessed by, the climax of erotic fever are to be found in the marmoreal concisions of Racine: in Nero's glimpse of his torchlit prey, in the quasi-monosyllabic parting of

Titus and Berenice, in Phaedra's maddened appropriation by "the entirety of Venus." The vehement pressure of sexuality in Baudelaire's sapphic poems, in Verlaine's *Stupra,* emanates from classical sources and a Latinate vocabulary. Lechery is almost rhetorical. It is linguistically choreographed as in the macabre *pas de deux* of Genet's *Maids.* And it is just this verbal formality which endows Sade's masturbatory lucubrations with their chill. In the vortex of pain and perversion—"there is paradise in that Hell"—none of the torturers or victims commits any grammatical error or lapses into inarticulacy. The radical pornography in French literature and imaginings is often that of loathing. Its supreme inventiveness spews out of the delirious pages—they altered, they infected the reaches of the language—of Céline's novels and leviathan "pamphlets." French sensibility harbors a black secret: hatred can be more warming, more orgiastic than love. It is precisely that "I do not hate you" which concedes, which enfranchises passionate love in a celebrated moment in Corneille's *Cid. Odi et amo,* inseparable.

The anatomical, neurophysiological mechanics of lovemaking (how risible they may seem at a distance) are common to all mankind. It is my thesis that both at their upper edge and at great depths, cultural, historical, social, contingent factors, such as circumcision, intervene. These qualify, differentiate and reshape universals. Of these variants, language seems to me to be the most influential and demonstrable. We speak love as we make it, both inwardly and outwardly. If French brings into performative play a distinctive formality and bias to abstraction, it also deploys, in regard to eros, a "naturalism" all its own.

Thus the French ethos is wonderfully receptive to the adult banalities, which are also essential truths, of human sexuality. Men will sleep with women, women with men, men and women with each other, because intercourse is overwhelmingly a bodily function, a *"call of nature."* The imperatives of the libido unfold beyond good and evil, as do human breath or the need for nourishment, those *nourritures terrestres* hymned by Gide. Men and women will sleep with each other outside the confines of marriage. Monogamy over a lifetime is a rare abstention from the obvious. The notion of sinful adultery belongs to an historical-theological code which French sentiment has ironized or ignored from the earliest *fabliaux* to the present. Observe with what didactic malice language inserts "adult" in "adultery"; it is not some punitive fiction of "impurity" which matters, but "adulthood." In a good marriage, sexual drives will wane with time, desire will stale. The magical modulation is that toward friendship. There is that in the latent violence and acrobatics of intercourse which becomes more and more alien to the genius of friendship as it can ripen between man and wife. Hence the ambiguous largesse of the designation *mon ami(e),* which, as in German *Freundin,* can signify either "mistress" or "friend," or that infinitely nuanced transit from one to the other. Anglo-Saxon intimations of puritanism, the fears and inhibitions they betray, the stain of prurience which marks American religiosity have been baffling or adverse to French consciousness across the centuries.

Arcane learning, the autistic minutia of specialized erudition can trigger a need for infantile release. S. had concocted a game of byzantine intricacy, part Scrabble, part strip poker. Sexual terms, some dating back to Old French, were to be defined and inserted in appropriate combinations. Two points each for *dard, lance d'amour, manche* or *nerf. Foutre* or *chevaucher* were too commonplace to merit more than half a point. Three points for *trou mignon* or *trou velu,* a bonus for the proper construal of *enfiler* and *la petite cuisson.* After which, in various stages of undress, S. would prepare one of the Breton dishes of whose sea-brine tang or touch of cognac she was past master.

The joyous or melancholy acceptance of love, even at its lyric pitch, as bodily function, anchors the French erotic glossary in a prodigal matrix of visceral components. Health, food and sex are enmeshed. In my prolonged liaison with N., digestion, migraine, rheumatism, constipation, allergies (mostly fantasized) played a prominent role. At moments, I had the impression, so vivid in Molière, of inhabiting, of copulating in a pharmacy. Syrups, sedatives, laxatives waited by the bedside. What may be the richest amorous vocabulary in Western literature, that of Rabelais, teems with medical and metamedical terms and allusions. Its brusque drollery and unabashed vulgarity are those of the hospital ward. Céline, too, was a physician drawing fiercely on medical candour as a legitimate conduit into obscenity. Via gastronomic voluptuousness and the price which the body pays, in defecation, nausea, vomit and obesity, Rabelais's language and that of his successors, such as Zola, dwells on every aspect of conspicuous alimentary consumption. "A nation of three hundred cheeses," complained de Gaulle sarcastically. But whose obverse is a heightened awareness in art, literature and social thought, of hunger. Where both gluttony and starvation saturate the *argot* but also the poetics of desire. *Mon brioche, mon brioche,* stuttered N. when nearing climax. Having, he claimed, made love during three days and nights, Zola staggered into the street enwrapped in the odor of sperm and that of freshly-baked bread, warm and golden as was his lover's cunt at daybreak.

There is, I believe, a philosophic-political core to this structure of consciousness (*mentalité*). Fucking is *liberty* in essence. It is the enactment and experience of liberty at its most absolute. Other languages have borrowed from French the expressions *libertin, libertinage*. In these, of course, *liberté* is declared. Insightfully, French grammar, myth and iconography feminize freedom. She strides toward us, triumphantly topless, in Delacroix's tumultuous allegory of revolution (note the phallic drumsticks). When they are in each other's arms, lovers exercise human choice, existential liberty as in no other act except suicide. There can be economic, social coercions, the blind lash of unreason, but at the heart of adult sex freedom exults. It reclaims from the banalities, from the servitudes of daily existence an inviolate space of possibility. It is one of the abjections of rape, of eros enforced, that it abrogates this space, that it enslaves. There is no more humiliating incarceration (cross-reference: Proust's *La Prisonnière*). But where it is lived freely, love and its sexual fulfillment emancipate the human spirit and bring it home to the enigma of the human body, of the body's determinant yet enigmatic weight in the realization of the self. No other phenomenality in our means can match or surpass this enfranchisement. *Liberté, liberté chérie,* proclaims the national anthem in a loving, amorous flourish. As sexual potency withers with age, as anxious onanism returns to substitute for coitus, freedom regresses. In this exact sense, old age is serfdom. Yet even here, remembrance can liberate. Those "snows of yesteryear" still gleam. The man, the woman who have known sex at its most various and unashamed retain the taste of freedom even to the end. One night in Paris, as I entered C., I heard the soft but meteoric laughter of liberty itself. It stays with me.

The global saturation by Anglo-American language(s), temporary as it may turn out to be, their dynamic geographical, ethnic, social variants, render any individual testimony, however promiscuous, minimal and unrepresentative. How can any one person register more than an insignificant fraction of a sexual lexicon and grammar which stretch from the syncopations of Afro-Carribean pidgeons to the delicate love lyrics of Anglo-Bengali, which comprise the créole of English hybrids in Southeast Asia and the worn passwords of the multinational dealer summoning his escort service to an anonymous hotel room in Istanbul or Valparaiso? Linguists estimate more than a hundred varieties of "English" current between the top of Manhattan and the outer reaches of Long Island. What unifies, what divides the sex slang of Bronx Yiddish and the American-fuelled *interlingua* of planetary pornography?

Amateurish intuition—"amateurish" does encapsulate "lover," *amatore*—suggests that American English, which is itself a reductive abstract, demythologizes. It distrusts, it subverts allegoric, symbolic indirections and circumlocutions as these have informed the discourse of eros in, say, Petrarchan diction or the sublimities of romanticism with its Neoplatonic origins. Operative, virtually ingrained in the American thesaurus of sex is a drive toward concreteness, toward graphic informality. The silences of Puritanism, the obliquity and the metaphoric in pre-Freudian proprieties have succumbed to "a frankness as never before" (Ezra Pound's phrase). Even Henry James's convoluted decorum, which, for a time, subsisted in homoerotic codes, has been effaced. Nakedness lies naked to language in a logical reversion to pre-Adamic innocence, to that prelapsarian Eden which is the quintessence of the American dream. The speech of desire and possession is at once secularized and without sin. It is at once disenchanted and infantile, "baby talk" in the sense in which all postponements of adulthood are Edenic. Paradoxically, it is the interminably repetitive exhibitionism and fraudulence of the pornographic which seek to insinuate into a neon-lit world the lost mythologies and frissons of the illicit. In everyday practice, for even "perversion" now looks to be a somewhat archaic, discriminatory pretense, spades are called spades and cunts cunts. Paraphrase is waste also in an economic sense. Waste of time and of libidinous opportunities. Mythology delays and complicates. It luxuriates. These are expenditures of feeling and of time alien to an American climate and its planetary export.

It follows that tides of populist and commercial detergence have rendered the concept of taboo virtually meaningless. With the language of the American military during and after the Second World War, came the universality of the expletive. "Fuck" and "shit" can punctuate every ordinary sentence. They have shed even the faintest aura of intimacy, of clandestine stimulus or inhibition. They are "fillers," nothing more. This deconstruction of impropriety, this abolition of subterranean or in any way demonic potency, has spread to wherever English and its multitudinous derivatives are in use. Certain vestiges of class demarcations in British English subsist. Here also, however, a democratization, a vulgarizaton of sexual speech acts is in rapid progress. The nonchalant, brutal candor of West Indian or Jamaican lingos across London and the Midlands, the derision in hip-hop and rap for what remains of bourgeois prissiness are sweeping aside ancient taboos. There is a raucous but also joyously truthful democracy of orgasm.

As I have indicated, this has brought with it an unprecedented standardization in the saying and making of love. American adolescents are thought to initiate and develop their sexual relations in accord with ritualized clichés both verbal and gestural. These and the cadence they activate stem from the proposals and icons of the mass media. The resulting vocabulary of lust and satisfaction, of coyness and seduction, is narrowly circumscribed. The resources of the language are used predictably. To a greater or lesser degree, such reductive uniformity and impoverishment extends into adult sexuality. Here also, the enunciation and enactment of love are too often prepackaged. They draw heavily on the plasticine rhetoric of film, of television, of pulp fiction and, above all, of commercials. At any moment in history, in any cultural milieu, singularities, neologisms of erotic expression are rare. In the American cadre of democratized libido and publicized consumption, innovations, genuine addenda to the executive means of sexual encoding, require genius. Such as we find in Nabokov's *Lolita* or at stellar occasions in the fiction of Updike. Tellingly, moreover, Nabokov made his sovereign entrance from outside the native tongue. Much of the rest is now texting, oral or electronic.

It will be fascinating to discover what complications and enrichments may come of feminist currents. These have produced powerful poetry and angry prose. Will their politics of feeling occasion new directions and creativity in the dialects of love? So far, the indications are marginal. What seems to prevail among emancipated women is the adaptation, almost contemptuous, of what were obscenities and clandestine license in masculine speech. The distinguished woman academic sitting next to me in a tedious colloquium scribbles on her notepad: "Wouldn't it be more fun if we fucked?" "Shit," exhales the woman driver as her motor stalls. As yet difficult to make out are the insinuations of lesbian parlance into the erotic mainstream. These may prove to be innovative. It is too early to tell. Long-suppressed and socially censored libidinal articulacy may surface as women assume equality and even take the initiative in the negotiations and performance of sex. As their vaginas master more than "monologues" couched as yet in primarily male accents and terminology. In Tulsa, Oklahoma, my glorious ebony partner hummed at me: "Baby, you haven't seen anything yet."

I have been privileged to speak and make love in four languages. Also in the interstices, sometimes inhibiting, sometimes playful, between them. This may be a somewhat unusual range. Heterosexuality has cut me off from vital realms and all manner of sunken treasure. The generative reciprocities between the linguistic and the sexual, "oral sex" in its fundamental sense, are, I am persuaded, a crucial but largely unmapped sphere. The inquiries to be made by cultural and social history, by psychology and comparative linguistics, by poetics and neurophysiology, are both extensive and difficult. Where it is obtainable, evidence tends to be anecdotal and impressionistic. Semantic Don Juanism remains a terra incognita waiting to be traversed and explored. Perhaps shared orgasm is an act of simultaneous translation. I sense that I could have made a contribution, even pioneering. But the hurt it would have done to that which is most precious and indispensable in my private life (this chapter comports risk) made this impossible. Indiscretion must have its limits.

| ZION |

WHAT THINKING WOMAN or man does not, at times in their lives, seek to arrive at a clear image, at a verifiable concept of their own identity? To ask "who am I" is a primary reflex in human consciousness. "Can I define myself to myself" and, either in immediacy or indirection, define myself to others? Do these two modes of self-definition coincide, or is there between them an insuperable gap? What "I," which "ego" is conceptually and existentially implicit in the assertion, philosophical or routine, internalized or declared, that "I am" or, more precisely, that "I am I," a finding always vulnerable to the challenges of schizophrenia, of autism or dementia? The Cartesian *ergo sum* finesses an inherent uncertainty. It is a boast rather than a self-evident truth.

It is my hunch that for Jewish men and women, where the mere term "Jewish" bristles with resistant complications, both this self-questioning and inquiry at large take on a specific edge. It is given only to the God of Moses to certify beyond doubt "I am that which I am" (translation wavers). The relations of a Jew to his or her identity can be so opaque, so stressful and replete with historical, social, and psychological ambiguities, that these define, if definition is allowed to include undecidability, the very condition of Jewishness. Nomination, guaranteeing real substance and real presence, is one of God's initial donations to Adam: "And whatsoever Adam called every living creature, that *was* the name thereof." A fantastic power to enforce truth-functions. The fall of man into the morass and license of the indefinite, into the gaps, which are often a chasm, between word and object, between name and essence, is the first exile. To a greater or lesser extent, all human beings share this ostracism, and numerous mythologies reflect it. Original sin is incised in grammar. In the experience of the Jew, however, this exile assumes a determinant role. For a Jew, self-consciousness, a balancing act difficult to achieve or sustain, comports banishment or, rather an endeavor, often desperate, to achieve some mode of homecoming. Adorno put forward a profoundly Jewish maxim whereby no man or woman who feels at home is at home. To which, inceaseless pendulum motion, Samuel 2:14 replies: "neither does God respect *any* person, yet does He devise means that His banished be not expelled from Him." *His* banished—a proud nuance. The exact discrimination between "banishment" and "expulsion" characterizes the space in which Jewish history transpires. If the God of Israel is, by exultant definition, *everywhere,* there can be no ontological expulsion from His presence. But there can, within this ubiquity, be banishment. From oneself first and foremost. More, perhaps, than any other ethnic, social or indeed mythological type, the Jew can be a stranger to himself or herself. His famed wandering is the allegorical-empirical representation of a search, of an incessant peregrination inward. He or she is alien to himself, to herself, before being alien to others. These, in turn, flinch from such unhousedness. It carries a strange, enervating aura. Consciously or not, the Jew is, in the deepest vein, restless. In what other faith, in what other canon, could we find the injunction: "Love not sleep" (Proverbs 20:13)? A summons whose enormity, whose singularity should not be taken lightly. Freud will despoil what remains of slumber of its innocence. He too, like the Jewish seers before him, was "a watchman in the night."

Anyone who regards himself or herself as "Jewish"—where "regards" can comprise numberless shadings of pride or of shame, of witness or concealment, of authenticity or factitiousness, of risk or of opportunism—must ask an initial and basic question: Why has the self-designation and designation from without of certain communities and individuals as "Jews," however contentious it is, endured? What meanings can attach to the survivance of this identification across more than three millennia? Other ethnic constellations and societies, collectivities no less distinctive, no less endowed, have perished. Why is there "Jerusalem" when Egyptian Thebes, Periclean Athens and imperial Rome have become archaeology? How can there be Jews still (the apposite Greek and theological word is "scandal")?

To the believing reader of the Torah, to the literalist who includes Christians faithful to Scripture, the answer is manifest. It is set out, immensely in Genesis 22:17–18: "I will multiply thy seed as the stars of the heaven, as the sand which is upon the seashore . . . And in thy seed shall all the nations of the earth be blessed." It is a breathtaking promise, consequential beyond words. It is for the believer an insurance and re-insurance on life itself. What man heard or wrote these words? If God was truthful unto Abraham—and how could He not be?—no massacres, no Shoah, no deportations, no scattering to the black and murderous winds, can extinguish the Jew. So long as God is, there shall be Jews. They will rise from their ashes to multiply again, to reclaim Zion. Their inheritance is a contract such as has been bequeathed unto no other people. Soon, there may be on the planet as many Jews as there were prior to the Shoah. In some respects, this is a numbing impropriety, in others it is simply an ineluctable legacy of God's promise to the patriarch. Other faiths, other nations succumb to time and to destruction. Not Judaism. Not this small, sharp-edged pebble in the shoes of mankind. "In this day will I raise up the tabernacle of David that is fallen, and close up the breaches thereof; and I will raise up his ruins, and I will build as in the days of old" (Amos 9:11). Again, this overwhelming promise of God to his hounded, powerless servant Israel. As absurdly improbable and "counterfactual" as it was by the waters of Babylon or in the Nazi death camps. A promise against all odds and reason. But *fulfilled*.

This is the riddle posed to the nonbeliever, to the rationalist and agnostic, to those who read the Hebrew Bible as an assemblage of folk myths, archaic ritual, tribal propaganda, absurdly minute dietary provisions and inspired moral and metaphoric imaginings. Who, from Spinoza onward, have felt it to be a thoroughly human production, riddled with contradictions and by no means innocent of ferocities (cross-reference: the book of Joshua). Yet no reasoned skepticism, no textual criticism can ever disprove, refute, or nullify the pact of survival set out in the book of Moses, celebrated in the Psalms and the Prophets. The forces of rational rebuttal, however informed by anthropology and editorial deconstruction, cannot refute what believers, and they need not be fundamentalists, take to be the word of God albeit qualified by human speech and finite understanding. Thinkers such as Leo Strauss have found this enigma of irrefutability to be both vibrant and insoluble. Revelation is not vulnerable to reason. So far, and against unspeakable odds, history has been on the side of the biblical message. After Auschwitz, Zion is being rebuilt. There *are* Jews.

But what makes them so? This turns out to be an exceedingly difficult and contentious question. Sartre's answer that it is the anti-Semite who defines the Jew is an adroit half-truth, entirely consonant with the dictate of one of Vienna's Jew-hating mayors: "It is I who decides who is or is not a Jew." For the Orthodox, the matter is obvious. A Jew, a veritable Jew, is one who observes the several hundred ritual, liturgical ordinances, prescriptions, prohibitions, dietary and vestimentary statutes which regulate every hour, every conceivable circumstance and demand of daily life from Sabbath to Sabbath. It is one, primarily male, who "shall order the lamps upon the pure candlestick before the Lord continually" (Leviticus 24:4); who will not eat "the little owl and the great owl, and the swan" (Deuteronomy 14:16); who knows that no iron tool may be used when erecting to God an altar of stones (Deuteronomy 27:5); and who understands why in matrimony the wife must take constant care not "to afflict the soul of her husband" lest he make their marriage void (Numbers 30:13). To the which prodigality of Mosaic and Levitical commandments, Talmudic interpretations and *Halachic* (normative, juridical) tradition have appended a legion of practices and formulaic pronouncements. In some essential manner, observance weighs more than belief, for it sets the Orthodox Jew apart, untainted by the gentile world. To the "liberal," to the modern Jew, let alone to the outsider, many of these injunctions and taboos seem little short of absurd. As do the almost hysterical mien and gestures of worship, of interminable and monotone recitation in the Orthodox school and house of prayer. What has he in common with the fanaticized, black-robed pack throwing stones at him out of the sanctity of the ghetto?

Unquestionably, however, it is the Orthodox Jew, in his Jerusalem or Williamsburg fastness, who is most at home in his identity, who dwells most securely in the promise made unto Abraham, who is patient but confident in expectation of the Messiah. It is he, his wife, their flock of children who leave the ritual bathhouse at sundown on Friday, their clothes shining with renewal, their faces lit as are those of no Jews of compromise. It is the Orthodox who are least in danger of assimilation. It is precisely strict observance, not speculative assent, which guarantees the election and survival of the Jewish people. It is not, awesome paradox, belief in God, but a daily reading of the Torah, or the refusal to violate fasting when dying of starvation. He who knows but does not query the precept that no man who is "broken-footed or broken-handed" may approach the tabernacle to offer bread to his God (Leviticus 21:19) will never be apostate, whatever the seductions of tolerance or of common sense. This pragmatic literalism is profoundly clairvoyant. Identity, familial and communal, is composed of shared motions and reiterations, not of philosophic abstractions or privacy. Assured faith is a style of life.

The cost, however, can be ominous. Like other fundamentalists, the Orthodox cultivate contempt for, even destestation of, the outsider. They hold in abjection the reformed Jew. Those who inhabit Israel condemn the state as it has not been validated by the Messiah. An Orthodox mob, seeking to annul by intimidation or violence some touch of secular freedom, is a parody of Jewish ethical-philosophical values while, at the same time underwriting the wonder of survival. To the Orthodox, gesticulating in front of the (mythical) Temple wall or plaguing the tourist with strident calls to repentance, a Spinoza, a Freud are as alien, as insufferable—in fact, more so—than their persecutors out of Christianity and Islam. The Orthodox and the Muslim fundamentalist are first cousins. But it was Orthodox rabbis and their acolytes who sang the Psalms both of mourning and of jubilation on the edge of the death pits.

For the "reformed," the "liberal," the occasional Jew who may, once a year, mark the High Holidays in filial piety, for the Jew ignorant of Hebrew or the atheist Jew, the issue of identity is thorny. More and more Jews, notably in the climate of acceptance or indifference in the United States, seep away from the issue altogether. Intermarriage is the open door into amnesia. It is solely when some anti-Semitic venom spurts, say in regard to their children in school, that such secular, non-observant Jews wake to their condition. This is the grain of truth in Sartre's thesis. Given the manifold permutations, always shifting, of non-Orthodoxy and self-marginalization, what common, binding factor can be demonstrated in today's Judaism?

Since antiquity, the notion "race" has adhered fatally (*fatum*) to the destiny of the Jew. In significant part, this fixation originates from within Judaism itself. The claim of being "a chosen people," an ethnic cluster set apart in singularity, is asserted by the Pentateuch and reaffirmed at key points throughout the Hebrew scriptures. This claim has incensed other peoples and nations. Jewish sages and moralists have laboured to assuage this resentment by characterizing "chosenness" in a tragic, almost masochistic light. God has singled out the Jew not for vainglory or envy but for perennial affliction. The Jew has been His chosen lightning rod, the scapegoat elect for His exasperation with sinful, mutinous mankind. Yet even this somewhat forced reading does not lessen the resentment of the Jew's self-declared apartness, of the pride which he, sometimes ostentatiously, takes in sorrow. He will not enroll in the commonplace, where the composition of that word deserves notice. Does this psychic and emblematic "racism" have any conceivable basis in biological facts? Is there, whether self-defined or invoked by others, any such thing as a Jewish "race"?

The lunatic, homicidal resort to a racial classification under Nazism and throughout the bestial history of pogroms and expulsion, has made any disinterested discussion of this question virtually impossible and indefensible. "Racism," however metaphoric, is inadmissible rubbish. Moreover, insist modern biology and genetics, the mere concept of racial purity or impurity is nothing but dangerous nonsense. There *may* be small ethnic pockets, insular and long isolated, whose genetic inheritance might exhibit a certain degree of invariant heredity. Even this is by no means certain. Rejection by other communities, a strong bias to endogamic marriages, concentration within circumscribed spaces or castes, *may* preserve and transmit an identifiable gene pool. Such identification is, however, highly dubious. Only a susceptibility to certain specific diseases seems to provide any substantive evidence. Even a ghetto is accessible to hybrid generic input. Across millennia, and via the interactive symbiosis of migration, Jews have, like other peoples, become "mixed." Political-legislative measures which aim to untangle this mixture, to determine exact fractions of Jewish "blood" and parentage reflect the madness, the inverse tribalism and neuroses of the Spanish Inquisitor or the fascist thug. As do scenarios, again dating back to classical antiquity, which would attach to Jews distinctive bodily traits (that notorious "Jewish nose"). There are blond, blue-eyed Jews as there are dark-skinned and hirsute ones. What alleged genetic, lineal unison relates the Jew out of Morocco to the Jew in Lithuania? What is there in common between Maimonides and the gangsters of Odessa, between Max Baer the heavyweight boxer and spectral Kafka? Intermarriage in today's agnostic West accelerates hybridization. Almost effortlessly, young American Jews can slip out of their historical and familial legacy. After a generation or two, their sometime Judaism is a blurred memory, a vestige of folklore. More than ever, there is no tenable justification for any definition of Jews as a race. Amen.

And yet.

I enter here on terrain of utmost fragility. Whatever argument can be looked at is bound to be intuitive and tentative. It will be unavoidably personal and composed of a mosaic of narrative and impression. Is there a "Jewishness" which is not contingent on historical circumstance and social milieu, which results from behavioural reflexes or recorded traditions, largely mythological? Is there something deeper? The question not only provokes disputatious unease, for it is also that of the anti-Semite. It may, in the final analysis, prove to be unanswerable.

So far as can be demonstrated, only one other major community, that of the Chinese, speaks a language which despite historical changes and accretions is that of its known origins. A source-language. Hebrew constitutes the axis and vital fabric of Judaism across millennia. One is tempted to equate the survival of the Jew with that of Hebrew, a survival reaffirmed by the renaissance of the language in Israel. The genius of the language empowers, incarnates the relations of the Jew to himself, to fellow Jews, but primarily to God. The classical Greek definition of human beings as "language animals" (*zoon phonanta*) is antithetical to Judaism. It divides Athens from Jerusalem. It is speech which, in the Judaic conception, makes women and men ontologically unique, which separates them from the animal kingdom. It is the unfathomable gift of language bestowed on Adam which makes possible, which compels consciousness and response in the face of God. It is the dialogue with a present or absent deity, where "dialogue" does not guarantee reply, which determines the history, the inherited identity of the Jew. "Hear me, God." "Listen unto me, Israel." The crucial case is vocative. But in far more than a grammatical sense. Hebrew is a calling by, a summons from, an address to God. Commandment and prayer are inseparable from an imperative of communication. At times, Hebrew almost breaks under the stress of incessant vocation: "I am weary of my crying: my throat is dried" (Psalms 69:3). But unquenchably the voice erupts, blazes anew: "Hear my voice, O God" (Psalms 64:1). In thanks, in jubilation, in awe. But also in lament, in bewilderment and reproach. What other people has been as incensed with its god? "Dost thou well to be angry?" asks God of Jonah in what one construes to be gentle irony. The "calling out," as the phrase is used in a duel of God in Job is like no other in world literature. As is the titanic irrelevance of God's riposte. It is anything but an answer: "Does the hawk fly by this wisdom and stretch her wings toward the south?" (Job 39:26). As if God reveled in His own incomparable rhetoric, in His virtuosity of metaphor. (What mortal being composed these chapters, and then went off to lunch?) If extinction was visited on Hebrew, as it has been on thousands of other tongues no less resourceful, no less eloquent, if silence interposed between God and the Jews, Judaism itself would cease. The Shoah hounded Judaism to the ashen edge of silence. But the language endured. In an abyss of inversion, it was now the Jew who prayed not *to* God but *for* him. Paul Celan tells us that in his Psalm:

> *Gelobt seist du, Niemand.*
> *Dir zulieb wollen*
> *wir blühn.*
> *Dir*
> *entgegen.*

Even on a lighter note, Judaism is a conversation with God. "Why did the Almighty bother to create men?" asks the Hassid: "So that they could tell Him tales."

Even Jews who lack Hebrew, a condition, I suspect, at the source of recurrent self-doubt, have shown a particular immersion in language(s). It is more than exile and the need to acquire the tongue of strangers which accounts for the linguistic gifts of the Jew. For his capacity to make of the affliction at Babel a harvest. There is even among agnostic, secularized Jews, among Jewish spokesmen for modernity, an intimation that identity is discourse, a discourse whose ultimate sanction is that of the articulate voice out of the Burning Bush and the whirlwind. The Jewish comedian, the Jewish impresario of mass communication and the media, the Jewish linguist—from Roman Jakobson and Walter Benjamin to Noam Chomsky and the negation of Derrida—relate, like spokes in a great wheel, to the centrality of the word. They testify to the pivot of the speech act, to a covenant between being and meaning. Despite its *scriptural* genius, despite its originating sovereignty over other poetic, narrative, visionary, legislative genres—a sovereignty unsurpassed and without which Western literatures are difficult to conceive—the Hebrew Bible is the record, certainly reductive, of an *oral* life-form. It encodes, with more or less economy and generalization, a record, a recollection of direct speech. Agony and prayer, celebration and lament, commandment and rebellion are *spoken*. We hear, precisely because Hebrew embodies the wonder and burden of audition, those letters of fire dictated to Moses on Mount Sinai, those words of retribution that blaze on the walls of Nebuchadnezzar's palace. In turn, Zionism is graven in the syntax of the Hebrew verb. Grammatically and metaphysically, Hebrew does not dissociate past present and future. Futurity is of the present. This is the very literality and paradox of the Messianic. Dispersed, all but eradicated, the Hebrew language never ceased proclaiming a wildly implausible return to its native ground. It made manifest the formal and existential means of rebirth. Today, Israeli novelists and poets are the contemporaries of, the transformative heirs to the Psalmist and the Prophets. "Next year in Jerusalem" is now. Of what other tongues, of what other nations can this be said?

The surprising turn is this: "voiced" into being, sustained by an uninterrupted vocal commerce with its God, Jews became "the people of the Book." This cliché is emphatically meaningful. It defines a lasting authenticity. Addiction to textuality has characterized, continues to characterize Jewish practice and sentiment. The tablet, the scroll, the manuscript and the printed page become the homeland, the moveable feast of Judaism. Driven out of its native ground of orality, out of the sanctuary of direct address, the Jew has made of the written word his passport across centuries of displacement and exile. It served as his refuge and indestructible abode. Hence the ordinance stated by certain rabbis that a daily reading of the Torah is of greater importance than love of God as it encompasses that love. Moreover, it underwrites, a telling idiom, the actual survival of the Jews. Clandestinely, Torah classes persisted to the very edge of extinction in the death camps. Necessarily, this immersion in writ engenders interminable commentary and commentary on commentary as if the margins and bottom of the page were the world. The Church Fathers, the Scholastics, will imitate this assembly line of secondary elucidation. But neither

Christianity nor Islam match the density, the torsions and filigree ingenuities of Talmudic exegesis and of the tertiary hermeneutics which the Talmud begets. As the Koheleth has it, there is in Judaism no end to the making of books and of books on books. Or as that literate politician Richard Crossman put it to me at the close of a debate: "a Jew is one who reads clutching a pencil because he is intent on writing a better book." More even than "sufferance," it is textuality and bookishness which have been "the badge of the tribe."

Saturation by commentary, by textualities parasitic on preceding expositions may, arguably, inhibit autonomous creativity. Nothing is more Jewish than Walter Benjamin's desideratum of a book made up solely of quotations. The Jew is an analyst, an expositor, at best a critic, not a creator, ruled Wittgenstein with irritated self-dismissal. There have been inspired poets among Jews and writers of Jewish provenance. Jehudah Halevi was only one among the constellation of Jewish poets in medieval Spain. One thinks of Heine, of Mandelstam, of Pasternak, or Paul Celan. Jewish masters of narrative came near to dominating American fiction in the later twentieth century. Dramatists such as Arthur Miller and Harold Pinter are Jews. Israel is producing novels and verse of the first rank. Intriguingly, a number of half-Jews have been among the classics: Montaigne, Proust. Is there a greater writer than Franz Kafka?

Nonetheless, the overall point has validity. It may be that the reasons are not far to seek. Such is the executive prodigality, the inventive scope of the Hebrew Bible that subsequent narrations or poetic and dramatic forms seem almost impertinent or, at best, gratuitious. How is any mundane writer to compete with, let alone surpass, the economies of Genesis, the epic sweep of Samuel and Kings, the eloquence of Jeremiah, the erotic music of the Song of Solomon or the proud pathos of the Psalms? What in any literature, be it *Gilgamesh* or Homer, reaches beyond David's lament over Jonathan or the hallucinatory prevision of the destruction of Jerusalem in the Prophets? What mortal text, it has often been asked, is not padded, is not in excess of its ideal self when set beside the twenty-third Psalm or the litany of the seasons in Ecclesiastes? But the crux may lie deeper. Read as divinely inspired, as echoing, though in ways perhaps hidden from us, the actual voice of God, these texts enunciate truths which render all literary writing fictive, which reduce it to belles lettres. Which insinuate into all other tales, poems, novels an organic falsehood and contingent opportunism. It was his unsparing confrontation of this possibility, his capacity to transmute it into parables which come close to the polysemic inexhaustibilities of their scriptural and Talmudic antecedents, which make Kafka incomparable. The "Parable of the Law" in *The Trial* is, perhaps, the only true addendum which secular literature has made to the Torah (it has been read as such in liberal synagogues).

En revanche, the textual proclivities of Judaism have produced masterly works of historical, philosophical, sociological, and scientific prose. What philosophical arguments do not seem inflated and somewhat dishevelled when compared to Spinoza or indeed Wittgenstein? Freud, Gershom Scholem rank with preeminent craftsmen of the German language. The case of Marxism and of Marxist socialism is the most striking. No political-social doctrine and program has ever been more bookish, more Talmudic in its tactics of debate. Marxism quotes incessantly. Its disputations, often literally homicidal, on the correct interpretations of Hegel, of the founding fathers, of Lenin, precisely mime the philological odium, the ad hominem rancour of rabbinic controversies. Trotsky was a brilliant publicist; even Stalin felt compelled to produce a learned monograph (by no means trivial). Modern psychology, social thought, social anthropology—consider the literary stature of Claude Lévi-Strauss—are at every point indebted to the textual immediacy of the Judaic tradition, to its instinctive appetite for normative clarity. As one Jew-hating Austrian politician put it: "Scholarship is simply what one Jew copies from another." When books are burned, a vital sinew in Judaism is consumed. Thus there is a logic of revolt in deconstruction whose acrobats are themselves so largely Jewish. Deconstruction is an attempt (Oedipal according to psychoanalysis) to overthrow the canonic weight of the text, to emancipate sense from patriarchal *auctoritas*. "Here we don't quote," shouted the Derridean mutineer in my lecture in 1968. Or as one (gifted) clown stated: "Language itself is fascist." For the Jew, textuality has been both survival and servitude, liberation and constriction. Ambiguity is there from the outset. What more haunting, prescient sentence than Koheleth 11:4: "He that observeth the wind shall not sow"?

Does this habitation in the written word relate to the considerable, some might say exceptional, contributions Jews have made to the life of the mind in both humanistic and scientific domains? Does it account for the widespread belief—expressed sarcastically, invidiously or in admiration—that Jews are "smarter," "brainier" or "cleverer" than their gentile neighbors? Whether there is any verifiable substance to these attributions remains difficult to assess. There *are* stupid Jews. There are subliterate Jews, though few. There are Jewish women and men innocent of any intellectual passion or cultural aspiration. It is, nevertheless, likely that Jewish intellectual energies are beyond random distribution or statistical probability. The proportion of Nobel laureates in medicine and the natural sciences as well as in economics far exceeds the norm. Jews have almost dominated certain branches of mathematics and of mathematical logic. With a handful of notable exceptions, they monopolize chess at its higher levels. They are everywhere present and prominent in musical performance. Only Darwin is the great "outsider" in the cluster of the shapers of modernity, of those who, like Marx, Freud and Einstein have become the "climate" of Western consciousness (Auden's expression). On an ancillary plane, the Jewish role in the media, in entertainment, in every aspect of international finance has been prodigious. Currently, the metropolis of cultural and financial dynamics, the talismanic *polis* which is New York, with Woody Allen as its bard, is also the capital of Judaism. These achievements and eminence have defied political oppression, social discrimination and outright massacre. Despite generations of Jew-hatred and relegation in the Russian empire and the Soviet Union, Jews have obstinately produced works of the first rank in Russian science, music and literature. Some primal force is at work.

Any attempt at diagnosis runs immediately and unavoidably into the debate over the respective causalities of genetic endowment, cultural inheritance and historical-social milieu. Barred from most normal ambitions, be they political, military or, for a very long time, academic (it was only after the Second World War that stringent quotas for Jews broke down in American higher education and medical schools), Jews were under pressures inward. Memorization, the discipline of analytic techniques, the cultivation of abstract and symbolic dialectics, were instrumental modes of shared experience in the Jewish quarter and its houses of prayer. Implosive cerebral acuities were compacted within confined social and pragmatic spaces. The central European *café* is the secular heir to the *Schul*. When emancipation, always grudging and qualified, came, this coiled spring of honed intellectuality burst outward. The reverence paid to the Talmudic master, to the scholar in the *shtetel*, the unbroken continuity of teaching, liturgical and secular, within the family—what other faith contains a formal blessing for the family which includes a scholar among its children?—modulated into the intelligentsia. It fueled the academic institutions, the free literacies, the laboratories in open societies. A long-enforced impatience now bore fruit. Heine is the incisive witness to this surge.

So runs the reasonable, the "politically correct" hypothesis. Is it wholly adequate?

Just now, the pendulum of argument is swinging markedly toward the genetic pole of the spectrum. Analysis has found a recurrence of highly specific traits and skills across distant generations. Medicine, social biology, ethnography are turning up more and more conditions in which genes do seem to outweight one's environment. As I pointed out, the mere concept of a Jewish gene pool conserved across time and admixture, is highly speculative, even suspect. None the less, we are dealing with a community which did live in considerable apartheid and which strove to exclude exogamy. It may, therefore, be arbitrary to avoid altogether the possibility of some measure of genetic inheritance, to disallow that there could be in specific lineages of Jewish excellence, but also in those of Jewish mediocrity or abstention, a biogenetic component. To the very end, Freud was a convinced, if partially covert Lamarckian. Today, the Lamarckian paradigm is emphatically rejected. No known somatic mechanism could account for it. Yet there is much we do not know. The suggestion of acquired characteristics hovers, like an ironic ghost, at the outer limits of scientific respectability and liberal good sense. Might it not be the better part of arrogance to admit that we know little about the generative interactions between nature and nurture, that there may be "illiberal" surprises in store? Late one night, during the bad years, I strolled outside my hotel in Kiev. A man caught up with me and asked in broken Yiddish: "You are a Jew, aren't you?" I asked him how he knew. "But surely it's obvious. The way you walk." Like one, I suppose, who has two thousand years of menace at his heels.

It was the wolfish, hypocritical dictates of Christendom which consigned the medieval and Renaissance Jews to usury. Which made Shylock typological. Yet there is more to it than that. Jewish intimacies with money have, in a sense, been visceral. They date back to the multiple fiscal prescriptions and motifs in the book of

Moses. As, perhaps, in no other mythology, money plays a canonic part in tales of good fortune and betrayal. The adroit pedlar is often identified with the Wandering Jew. He will graduate to being the informed trader, the merchant across frontiers, the banker and broker of capitalism. Whatever its ideological strata in Protestantism, the evolution of modern capitalism and the critique it has inspired find a natural context and adaptation in the Jewish community. It seems to enlist ancient skills and predispositions. The Rothschilds replace Shylock. From the late nineteenth century onward, Jewish assiduity and inventiveness in the money markets, investment banking, venture capital, and the bourse have been little short of paramount. The Jewish aristocracy, that of the Bleichröders, Rothschilds, Warburgs, and Lazards has been one of high finance. Firms such as Goldman Sachs or Lehman Brothers, individual alchemists such as George Soros, have been decisive players in fiscal mechanisms of the West. Multinationalism has recruited the peregrine, cosmopolitan instincts of the Jews. It "naturalizes" his condition. Thus, today, a significant percentage of global finance is under Jewish management. The analytic, metamathematical talents displayed by Jewish logicians and scientists have been brilliantly deployed in the domains, at once hyperrational and demonic, of money. Hence the consonance between the Diaspora and the exuberant economic impulses in American life. But also in postcommunist Russia, so many of the robber barons, of the billionaire entrepreneurs have mushroomed out of a long-despised, persecuted minority.

The dialectical counterpoint is equally striking. It is out of Judaism, from Amos to Marcuse, that spring the most radical, the angriest excoriations of the pursuit and idolatry of wealth. The deepest loathing of the Golden Calf. Socialism and communism of every tint are both doctrinally and historically permeated by Jewish values and presence. The prophetic, accusing rhetoric of Karl Marx, his Old Testament mien and iconography are Judaic to the core. Jews peopled the Menshevik and Bolshevik movements. In inheritance of Mammon, Jewish radicals, socialists, Marxists, practical or utopian, turn against riches. The left-wing *kibbutz* aimed to abolish altogether the regime of money, of pecuniary motives and rewards. Magnificently, Amos preaches the march of the ascetic, moneyless desert on the corrupt, wealth-sodden city. (Had Mao read these pages?) The Messiah will carry no cash.

From within capitalism itself, however, Jews have turned creatively, as it were, on their own financial success. They contribute, far in excess of any other ethnic group, to charity, to education, to cultural institutions, to medical care and research. American higher learning, hospitals, museums, symphony orchestras are significantly sustained by Jewish largesse. Were it not for Jewish generosity, often of immigrant origins, the financial situation of research and of the arts in the United Kingdom would be even more parlous than it is. Also in this respect, the exemplary ideals and commendations are biblical. Hebrew scriptures abound in injunctions to charity, to the succour of the destitute and the stranger. Surplus is to be redistributed, be it to the gleaners out of Moab. "In the year of this jubilee ye shall return every man unto his possession" (Leviticus 25:13). Compelled by hostile oppression, but also by deeply ingrained capacities to exercise financial and commercial skills of the most conspicuous order, Jews have always been haunted by the intimation of criteria, of social bonds prior to, untainted by, money. They give it away as if it clung pestilentially to their fingers. What is more Jewish than Marx's call, in the 1844 *Manuscripts,* for a society in which love will be exchanged for love, trust for trust, and not money for money? It is an ancient Jewish maxim that it is both defeat and folly to die rich.

There could well be other distinctive markings in which both environment and some form of heredity, as yet undeciphered, are operative. Jewish humor is a crowded chapter. It has a salt all its own, a bracing desperation. Its self-mockery tells of talismanic resistance to suffering, to exclusion. It is no accident that the only two worthwhile philosophic tracts on jokes should be by Freud and Bergson. All peoples cherish their children. In Judaism this focus often looks to be surpassing. Do other faiths encode as unforgivable any harm brought to a child—here Jesus of Nazareth is at his most Jewish. In the present anguished climate, criminologists report that pedophilia and child abuse are exceedingly rare among Jews. Dietary laws, originally hygienic and therapeutic, have left Jews, wherever they may be, with characteristic aversions. They have set Jews apart in the anthropologically crucial demarcations between pure and impure. Circumcision is now widely practiced. Did this usage, together with other taboos, afford its own tenor to Jewish sexuality? So many questions.

Of which the most pressing and intractable is that of constant anti-Semitism.

Can one unravel its underlying causes? Must it last forever?

Attempts to explain this cancer are legion. Historians adduce traces of Jew-hatred in Mediterranean antiquity. They discern in imperial Rome some of the attitudes which were to persist. Jewish apartness bred suspicion and worse. The Jews' refusal to observe the fairly benign formalities of civic and imperial ceremony exasperated their rulers and neighbors. An irritating theocratic snobbery seemed to attach to their refusal of assimilation. In the midst of syncretic ecumenism, the God of Israel scorned membership. Roman conquerors of Jerusalem recoiled from the blank emptiness of the holy of holies in the sacked temple. The abstraction of what were held to be Jewish beliefs (monotheism had, in fact, cropped up elsewhere) and the lack of public imagery generated malignant apprehensions. Here was an unyielding minority, a splinter among nations, in touch with occult agencies and hidden fonts of power. On the whole, however, hostility towards Judaea, even where it took on violent guise, was political and territorial rather than ideological. Tacitus documents this reflex.

All this changed with the advent and triumph of Pauline Christianity, that most consequential act of self-hatred in Jewish history. There followed the canonization of Jew-baiting passages in the Synoptic Gospels. Christianity could not forgive, it has never forgiven the refusal of the Jews to enter the *ecclesia* of their own free will. In some respects, this refusal, which accoding to Pauline theology holds all mankind hostage, does remain puzzling in view of messianic expectations and certain Old Testament apocalyptic previsions (perhaps, as Scholem sardonically remarked, Jews waited for a fortnight after Jesus's alleged resurrection and saw that nothing whatever had changed). The anger of the Church Fathers, of a nascent clerisy, at those who would not recognize in Christ the promised, the risen Messiah unleashed millennia of hatred and persecution. Anti-Semitism uncoiled on its venomous progress toward a "final solution." The continuities may be tortuous and sometimes occluded, but they are undeniable.

No record does justice to the long horror. Episodes, periods of particular persecution are notorious. They comprise the massacres at the time of the Crusades, the pogroms in eastern and central Europe from medieval to modern times, the expulsion from Spain and its hideous Inquisitorial aftermath, the innumerable instances of local killing triggered by the "blood libel" (bestialities still recalled with honor in rural Austria in the twenty-first century). But it is not explosive terror which tells the main story. It is the everyday condition of the Jew in a Christian world. Beyond computation, like the "dark matter" in cosmology, are the social ostracism, the extortions, the judicial discrimination, the derision to which Jewish women and men have been exposed even in relatively liberalized and formally tolerant communities. There can be no catalog of the times Jewish children have been chased down the street (I know about this sport first hand), spat on, or mauled on their way to and from school; of the occasions, public and professional, on which their parents have been patronized, insulted and shown the door. From childhood on, the Jew carries within him the sweat of fear. Only the Gypsies, it may be, have endured a comparable chronicle of rejection.

The madness of the Shoah, much in excess of understanding and narration, had its logic—as madness often has. Only total annihilation could terminate "the Jewish problem." Murder had to be ontological. Which is to say that it had to eliminate the fact of being. The Jewish fetus could no longer be allowed to come into existence. It had to be butchered together with its pregnant mother. In the Nazi slaughterhouse, the original sin of the Jew, the leprosy with which he threatened the gentile, was his mere being. Debates over the possible uniqueness of the Shoah are superficial and demeaning. Stalin did to death far more human beings than did Hitler. Millions of so-called *kulaks* and their families were deliberately starved to death for the crime of being *kulaks*. Armenians, Indonesians, and peoples of Somalia have been massacred en masse. What reliable account is there of the elimination of Aborigines in Australia, of genocide in the Belgian Congo (historians put the figure of victims at anywhere between five and ten million). *Homo sapiens* is a creature inclined to homicide, equipped for sadism. Statistically, the Holocaust will almost certainly not have been the worst chapter. Our earth is sown with killing fields.

Yet there *is* a difference. Which may be crucial. No ideology outside Hitlerism defined and proclaimed existence and survival as criminal. No other ideology and political program proclaimed openly that its purpose could not be achieved so long as one Jew, vermin though he was, endangered, in some pathogenic way, the existence of the non-Jew. Because the endurance of this loathed remnant could infect the blood and souls of their fellow men. Thus, from the Rhineland massacres and the pyres of the Inquisition to the gas ovens, the road is a twisting one. But it can be mapped. Penitential suavities in recent Vatican pronouncements have been largely cosmetic. The sense of the Jew as pariah is ingrained. "They have wandered as blind men in the streets, they have polluted themselves with blood, so that men could not touch their garments. . . . They hunt our steps, that we cannot go in our streets" (Lamentations 4:14–18).

Can there be any tenable explanation? For the fact that the Japanese, who have hardly ever set eyes on a Jew, are the constant publishers and distributors of the totally fraudulent but murderous *Protocols of Zion*? For the unquenchable Jew-hatred in Poland, in Austria, now that there are virtually no Jews left? For the resurgence of bitter anti-Semitism in postcommunist Russia and, currently, at flash points throughout western Europe? What night passes without the vandalization of a Jewish cemetery, even in benign Britain? "The tumult of those that rise against thee increases continually" (Psalm 74:23).

Why?

Historical, sociological, economic theories abound. Both autarkic and enforced, the apartness, the isolation of the Jew, his refusal, for so long a period, to melt into common humanity, has enervated and incensed the gentile. It has been a sharp bone in his throat. The excluder felt excluded, an inflammable brew. The abstention of Judaism from proselytizing, the barriers which it puts in the way of those who might want to enter the covenant, an eccentric but not altogether unknown impulse, worsened this sense of reciprocal ostracism. Only elimination, even in ominous remembrance, could resolve this nagging intuition of some transcendental arrogance. On an economic plane, Jews were moneylenders, however upright and coerced. Kill him, torch his counting house and your debts would be canceled. Unquestionably, this factor mattered in the pogroms, in the lust to harry Jews out of the land. With the flowering of Jewish good fortune in mature capitalism, which I have cited, jealousy of what seemed occult manipulative skills and foresight often grew hectic. Anti-Semitism achieved the deft trick of characterizing Jews as being simultaneously Bolsheviks and plutocrats. This duality figured large in Nazi myths.

Self-hatred, an intricate imbroglio, added its particular virus to the Jewish condition. It can be found among the most gifted, in Marx, in Weininger, at certain points in Wittgenstein, rabidly in Simone Weil. If such Jews could ironize and repudiate their heritage, why should the outsider not do so? To all this must now be added the dilemmas posed by Zionism, by the establishment of a militant state in Israel. Inescapably, the Jew in today's Diaspora is shadowed by the potential of divided loyalties. He is of the gentile community which he inhabits but, whether voluntarily and consciously or not, also of Israel. Where is his inward, final homeland? *To survive, Israel has had to become a nationalist, sometimes aggressive and repressive society.* It has had to be chauvinist in order to prevail against formidable odds. I will come back to this point. What is now patent is the use of anti-Zionism, itself a defensible option, to absorb and mask anti-Semitism of every nuance. It is becoming ever more difficult to separate the two. How much of the indictment of Israel by the Left, old and new, is basically Jew-hatred and self-hatred (Noam Chomsky's ungoverned denunciations of "Israeli fascism")? What sick ironies attach to the support which Israel attracts from the fanatical Right, from French proto-Nazis, or the fundamentalist congregations of the American South? In a more diffuse perspective, how much plausibility is there to the intimation, populist or educated, that our geopolitical world will find no rest, will arrive at no concord with Islam, so long as the fate of Israel destabilizes not only the Middle East but significant elements in the Diaspora, as in the former Soviet Union? What "rough beast," as Yeats intuited, keeps "slouching towards Bethlehem"?

All these elements and their complex aggregates do matter. Together, they have woven a suffocating web. The bind is double and treble as Jewish reactions to unending pariahdom reinforce the very traits which trigger anti-Semitism in the first place. The spiral is infernal. Yet even compounded and rationally assessed, do these circumstantial, material, psychic motives yield an adequate diagnosis? Can they, I repeat, account for anti-Semitism in countries where there have been no Jews or in which Jews have been all but wiped out?

I think not. Hence my resort to vulnerably metaphoric, to theological concepts.

A theological, Christological anti-Semitism is crucial to the inception of Christianity. "Blindness" shall be visited on Israel by virtue of its rejection of the crucified Christ. There can be no Second Coming, no ultimate salvation so long as Jews do not convert, a length of time which Andrew Marvell equated famously with eternity. Though attenuated by modern agnosticism, the deadly polemic remains. Seemingly powerless, dispersed, contemned, lamed, perhaps enduringly, by the Shoah, Judaism holds its great heresy and heir, Christianity, captive. Romans 11 allows no doubt: Only when a Christian God shall "graft the Jews in again" will wretched humankind accede to universal peace. What sign, however, is there of any such blessed integration? Of all the Apostles, by name and physique, by his association with money, it is Judas who is the arch-Jew. Two thousand years of Christian homily and propaganda, of Christian iconography, have labored the point. He is the unforgiven villain, with his red hair, hooked nose and pieces of silver.

I have tried to think further.

In and of itself, the charge of deicide which, over centuries, Christianity flung at Judaism, is demented. How can men kill God (albeit there may be, in the Eucharist, a practice repellent to Jewish feeling, some vestige of cannibalistic rites)? But however lunatic, the accusation that the Jews had "killed God" in the persona of his Nazarene son, rang down the ages. Howled by the looting mob, expounded by divines including Luther, this obscenity helped dispatch thousands of Jewish men, women, and children to hideous deaths. I have suggested, in previous work, that this denunciation in fact conceals the authentic indictment. By virtue of an inversion familiar to both mythology and psychoanalysis, the charge of deicide stands for its exact opposite. The Jew is hated not because he *killed* God but because he has *invented* and *created* Him.

Monotheism, as it evolved out of Abraham and the revelation on Mount Sinai put an unbearable moral and psychological burden on man. Early Judaism often rebelled against this intolerable weight. Polytheism, whether in its pagan forms or Trinitarian compromise, satisfies fundamental human needs and imaginings. Hence the undying spell of classical mythology. The notion of an unimaginable, unreachable, unnamable God, blank as the desert air, enraged by any sensory or even allegoric representation, is almost "revolting" (in both senses of that word) to common human sensibility. It is, in the literal sense, "unspeakable." Yet from this faceless infinity emanate ethical commandments, imperatives of right conduct, exactions of private and of social justice far beyond the reach of the vast majority of mankind. Omnipresent, omnipotent, implacable, the God out of Mount Sinai and the whirlwind is an unanswerable critique of natural man. It was the seductive genius of Pauline Christianity to invite human beings into the loving, forgiving, richly pictorial house of God via the sacrificial interposition of Christ. To recognize man for the "naked and forked creature" he is, while sanctifying that infirmity. The worship of Mary, the crowded pantheon of interceding saints, the mediations of art and music, closed to iconoclastic Judaism, rendered relations to a triune deity virtually domestic. All of which is alien to the humbling, disputatious, endlessly exigent abstractions of Jewish monotheism.

Twice more, Judaism or its immediate derivatives confronted

men with the blackmail of the absolute, with moral and social ideals foreign to human nature and capacities. The Sermon on the Mount is largely a transposition from a citation of the Prophets. When Jesus bids his followers to "take no thought for their lives," to forgive their enemies, to "judge not, that ye be not judged," to love their neighbors as they would themselves, he is rephrasing the teachings of Isaiah, the admonitions of Jeremiah. The altruism, the otherworldliness of the demands put by Jesus the Jew are sublime reproof to the mundane existence, to the egotism which impells our natural conduct. The closing sentence of the Sermon reads: "Be ye therefore perfect, even as your Father which is in heaven is perfect." Nothing less. This ordinance is, to put it carefully, little short of monstrous. A scattering of holy folk, of ascetics in fanatical solitude, have striven to enact this commandment. The normal woman or man pays lip service; they do not, they cannot, live their works and days in this blinding light. This failing, however, nurtures fierce psychological resentment.

The third instance of Judaic ethical exaction is that of utopian socialism, notably in the messianic guise of Marxism. Once more, mankind is asked, indeed ordered, to be better than itself, to liquidate its cupidities and petty pleasures, to share unstintingly with others, to merge egotism into the fate of a disciplined collectivity. Communism paid to men the compliment of an immense expectation. Carried out in certain revolutionary, sacrificial gestures, in some radical communes, it enforced a Spartan diminution of self, a visionary commitment far beyond our infirmities. Yet they are felt to be an ideal and the foundations of justice on an exploited, self-destructive earth.

Nothing breeds a deeper loathing than demands one cannot meet but which one recognizes, however fitfully or subconsciously, to be irrefutable. It is this loathing, this resentment, I believe, which underlies and perpetuates Jew-hatred. Hitler termed the Jew "the inventor of conscience." I would say: "of bad conscience."

I continue to believe that there is substance to this moral-psychological explanation and etiology of anti-Semitism. But I now find myself wondering at the provocation posed to the gentile world by the mere fact (that "scandal") of Jewish survival. With regard to the Chinese, overwhelming numbers provide a license and justification. The demographic insignificance of Jewish settlements, their repeated escape from annihilation are a "strangeness," and "enormity" unto themselves. They act like a fiery itch under the skin of the non-Jew. There is a fierce impertinence to Jewish survival. The relevant social, psychic configuration is difficult to define. Nonetheless, I find myself asking, with a deepening sense of urgency, what could render plausible, what could legitimize the quite fantastic fact with which this chapter began: Why are there still Jews?

The State of Israel gives a triumphant, at times triumphalist answer. A phoenix risen from the ashes, but with talons of steel. Its coming into being, its survival surrounded by deadly enemies, are a miracle. As is the clearing of the land, stone by stone, the foundation of a modern, highly educated democratic community, and its integration of a host of immigrants. Every Jew on this earth now has a guaranteed refuge. All these are wonders without a genuine parallel anywhere else in history. Israel marks both an ancient and an unprecedented miracle in Jewish destiny, in the possibilities of Jewish survival. But in order to be, Israel has had to regenerate capacities and values dormant since the book of Joshua. It has had to cultivate, to glorify military skills and ruthlessness. The internal cost has been considerable. Israeli society is of necessity militant and often chauvinistic. There is not always—how could there be?—either time or space or the economic means for those cultural, scientific, aesthetic pursuits which adorn the Diaspora. It is not in Israel that Nobel Prizes or philosophic creativity are thick on the ground. But it is early days, and this is not the crux.

Essentially powerless for some two thousand years, the Jew in exile, in his ghettos, amid the equivocal tolerance of gentile societies, was in no position to persecute other human beings. He could not, whatever his just cause, torture, humiliate, or deport other men and women. This was the Jew's singular nobility, a nobility that seems to me far greater than any other. I hold it as axiomatic that *anyone who tortures another human being, be it under compelling political, military necessity, that anyone who systematically humiliates or makes homeless another man, woman or child, forfeits the core of their own humanity.* The imperative of survival, the ethical ambiguities of its settlement in what was Palestine (by what sophistry does a nonbelieving, nonpracticing Israeli invoke God's promise to Abraham?), have forced Israel to torture, to humiliate, to expropriate—though often to a lesser degree than its Arab and Islamic enemies. The State lives behind walls. It is armed to the teeth. It knows racism. In short: it has made of Jews *ordinary men.* Demography in fact threatens this soiled normality. There will before too long be more Arabs inside Israel than there are Jews. Only catastrophe in the outside world could trigger a new inflow of immigrants. That the collapse of Israel would produce an irreparable psychological and spiritual crisis throughout the Diaspora is more than likely. But it is not certain. It may well be that Judaism is larger than Israel, that no historical setback could extinguish the mystery of its endurance. Christianity may have been strongest in the catacombs. We simply do not know. In the meanwhile, however, Israel is reducing Jews to the common condition of nationalist man. It has diminished that moral singularity and that aristocracy of nonviolence toward others which were the tragic glory of the Jew.

I know the inhuman cost which this omnipotent impotence entailed. I know how facile, how cheap it is to criticize Israel if one is unwilling to share its burdens and constant danger. Yet it is this sense of diminution which has prevented me from being a Zionist, from making my life and that of my children in Israel. Parlour-

Zionists are as contemptible a breed as were the fellow travelers lauding the Soviet Union but careful never to put a step within its borders.

The Diaspora is itself under threat. I have refered to the constant seepage of assimilation and intermarriage. Yet I believe intensely that for the Jew outside Israel, for a certain proportion of Jews outside Israel, survival signifies a mission. At key points in Mosaic law and Talmudic exegesis, the Jew is instructed to make welcome the stranger. He must never forget that he too was a stranger, an alien in the land of Egypt. That he too has been homeless and a refugee on an unwelcoming earth. It is my conviction that the Jew in the Diaspora must survive in order to be a *guest among men*. All of us are the guests of life, thrown into life beyond our volition and understanding. We are now being made grimly aware that we are the guests of a vandalized planet. Unless we learn to be one another's guests, mankind will slither into mutual destruction and perpetual hatred. A guest accepts his host's legislature and usages, but may labor to amend them. He learns the languages of his hosts, but may strive to speak them better. Above all else, he will, if he moves on, either freely or under compulsion, seek to leave his host's dwelling cleaner, more comely than he found it. He will endeavor (Spinoza's *conatus*) to add something of value, intellectual, ideological, material, to what he found when he came knocking at the door.

The arts of being a guest are frequently almost impossible to practice. Prejudice, jealousy, territorial atavisms on the part of the host pose a constant threat. However warm the initial welcome, the Jew does well to keep his bags discretely packed. If he is forced to resume his wandering, he will not regard this experience as a lamentable chastisement. It is also an opportunity. There is no language not worth learning. No nation or society not worth exploring. No city is not worth leaving if it succumbs to injustice. We are accomplices to that which leaves us indifferent. The password of

Judaism is *Exodus,* the spur of new beginnings, of the morning star. Hitler spoke derisively of *Luftmenschen,* of the Jew as an un-housed "creature of the air." But the air can be a realm of freedom and of light. "Be a fertilizer among men," urged one of the founders of Israel, "compacted into one nation you may become dung." Nationalism, of which Israel is necessarily emblematic, tribal ingathering, seems to me not only foreign to the inward genius of Judaism and the enigma of its survival. It violates the imperative of the Baal Shem Tov, master of Hassidism: "The truth is always in exile." This maxim is my morning prayer.

I realize full well that a peregrine state is not for everyone. That the risks it incurs are extreme. The Shoah may have made a mockery of my persuasion. Yet I repeat: Let us survive, if at all, as guests among men, as guests of being itself. At its festive table, the Jewish family keeps a seat vacant for the stranger who may come to the door. He may be a beggar or a veiled messenger from God. He must never be turned away. To be a host is also to be a guest. This is the defining purpose, the justification of the Diaspora.

I had hoped to hammer out these arguments is a full-scale work. I lacked the clarity of vision to do so.

And the Hebrew.

| SCHOOL TERMS |

REPEATEDLY, I HAVE been invited by the relevant services of
UNESCO, by the European Commission in Brussels, and by cultural foundations to prepare a comparative study of the ideals and
performance of secondary and higher education on the European
continent, in Britain, and in the United States. These invitations
arose from my own curriculum vitae. I have studied and taught
within each of these three systems. This may be an unusual exposure.

Born in Paris, brought up trilingually, I grew up in wartime
Manhattan where I first attended a highly regarded American high
school but then returned to the French *lycée*. My university years
took me to the University of Chicago, then in a stellar phase, and to
Harvard. After which, and in a somewhat anarchic vein, I completed my graduate training at Oxford. I taught at Cambridge and,
for a quarter of a century, at the University of Geneva in what is the
oldest recognizable chair of comparative literature (finely named
littérature générale). I have held visiting professorships at Princeton, Stanford, Yale and the Eliot Norton Professorship of Poetics at
Harvard. I am a founding Fellow of a Cambridge college and hon-
orary Fellow of two Oxford colleges. I have lectured at Glasgow
and at London University. At the Sorbonne and the Collège de
France. At the universities of Bologna and Siena and at the French
Academy in Rome. During the cold war decades, I visited eastern
European universities and academies and held seminars in East
Berlin (without the heroic fuss which later made such visits mod-
ish). I have taught at the magical university of Girona in Spain, in

China and Japan, and also in Johannesburg. Trinity College, Dublin, has been my host. Memories include those of audiences resolutely hostile during the student rebellions in Frankfurt and tumultuously responsive in the teeming Mexican universities. A semi-clandestine lecture on Kafka in strangled Prague remains a talismanic hour. Of late, I have lectured to and met with secondary school children whenever possible, notably in Italy. Theologians and philosophers have made me welcome in Copenhagen and in the ornate halls of Coimbra in Portugal.

This range reflects not only a polyglot condition and a life in motion, partially elective, partially brought on by historical pressures. It stems from my almost embarrassing passion for teaching and from the hybrid nature of my interests: comparative literature and the interface between poetics and philosophy, the charged spaces in which Plato challenges the poets and Paul Celan seeks out Martin Heidegger. Consequently, I have taught American texts in eastern Europe and the Far East, English classics in France or Italy, German romanticism in the United States. I have lectured on Lukács and Marxist hermeneutics, on moral-political critiques of the fine arts, in Gombrich's presence at the Courtauld Institute in London. Umberto Eco, the high priest of the trade, has allowed, with an amicable growl, that I may have be the only itinerant scholar (or certainly one of exceedingly few) to lecture, teach and publish in four languages. Again, the reasons are in part biographical, in part contextual to my training and professional options. But they do amount to a possible basis for comparative evaluation.

The obstacles, however, are formidable, perhaps insuperable. Within each of the three paradigms I was asked to consider the local variants are manifold. What is there in common between a rural high school in Arkansas, an inner-city school in Los Angeles, and a patrician academy in New England? Between a land-grant or junior college in Alabama and MIT? How can any generalization apply legitimately to comprehensive classes in Hull or Hackney and to Eton or Winchester? What, if anything, relates the school on the edge of a Sicilian slum to a renowned *liceo* in Pisa? The criteria of admission and certification vary widely between the monster-universities in the Ruhr and elect faculties in, say, Tübingen. Between populist urban campuses on the outskirts of Paris and the École Normale. Moreover, my personal experience as a student is dated; that of my teaching is beginning to be so. Changes have been all but cataclysmic in educational structures. What is now regarded as a crisis in educational standards throughout the Western world has unfolded rapidly. It follows on the larger crisis of successive world wars, of mass emigration, of Americanization and the erosion of traditional power relations in society. It is inseparable from the complex phenomenology of the decline of religion in a technological, mass-market era. In too many respects, I am already an archaic spectator. How is any serious comparative analysis to proceed?

Statistical surveys are innumerable. The graphics are impressive. But so much data is suspect and often ideologically motivated. Reportage, even by the best qualified, is unavoidably impressionistic and fragmentary. Theories and empirical practice, political platforms and executive realization quickly drift apart. Economic differences, social determinants, ideological and civic intentions not only divide public from private schooling. They generate complex eddies within an outwardly standardized construct. Girls and young women have only fairly recently been made welcome in English public schools or in university departments of science and engineering. Their chances as teachers in higher education have been slow to flower. The German situation remains forbidding, as it does in Italy. Gifted women are driven out of the profession or relegated to its margins. Add to this the electronic revolution, the exponential role of the computer, the Web, the Internet in every facet of schooling and literacy. I have, in a previous chapter, referred to what is a metamorphosis in the training and development of mental resources. The gap yawns between the pre-computer literate such as myself and the new age. Fundamental notions, modified only in part since classical antiquity in the West, are now, as it were, in transit. Memory was the mother of the Muses. How does this didactic myth relate to the memory banks of cyberspace? In the light of these changes and uncertainties, what realistic chances are there of a reliable, let alone comprehensive comparative inquiry?

I have long dreamt of organizing an international literacy and "general knowledge" Olympiad along the lines of the famous mathematics Olympiads. Selected students, from different age levels, would be invited to take uniform examinations, to compose essays on identical topics, and engage in viva voce challenges. These students would represent educational institutions in the Anglo-American sphere, and on the European continent, including Russia. The practical difficulties are considerable. Secondary and advanced training in different nations and different social hierarchies are so diverse that competition and comparison on equal terms looks to be well-nigh impossible (the universality, the objectivity of mathematical tasks and solutions largely removes this impediment). What skills other than the rudimentary are taught in common? Preliminary calibration and matching would need to be of the utmost precision and fairness. Could a sixth-former from a British school be matched against a pupil in the *première* of a French *lycée* and a boy or girl in the *Matura*-class of a German or Austrian *Gymnasium*? Conceivably, this could be managed at an elite level. Where less selective, less "academic" secondary education is enlisted, the obstacles to reciprocal concordance may be insurmountable. In the context of higher education, the barrier to just comparison seem less obvious. In fact, they are virtually as inhibiting. Despite shared ideals and exchanges, Oxbridge or the London School of Economics have no substantive counterpart in the American Ivy League or among the world-class institutions on the American West Coast. It is not the Sorbonne which embodies the cream of French higher learning and teaching: it is the *Grandes Écoles,* a unique constellation of Napoleonic centralizing measures and republican mandarinate. In both Italy and Germany, specific faculties, particular departments and even individual academic stars can represent excellence and selectivity within an often chaotic sprawl. Consider metaphysics in Tübingen, classics in Pisa or semiotics in Bologna. Collegiate and graduate pre-requisites and standards in all too many American colleges and universities verge on the vocational or worse. Subliteracies of every kind are allowed in establishments whose true purpose is one of civic integration. How is one to arrive at any equitable norm? Who would constitute an impartial jury? Again, mathematics enjoys the luxury of measurable certitudes.

None the less, I do find myself imagining a session of exams, composition, and oral response in which participants would be drawn from, say, Harvard, Stanford, and MIT; from Oxford, Cambridge, and Imperial College; from the École Normale and Polytechnique and that of Sciences Politiques; from among Munich's students of history and budding sociologists in Frankfurt; from Pisa's *Scuola Normale* and the best of students at the universities of Moscow and St. Petersburg. Add to these the delegates from adult and continuing education, from the *troisième âge,* who play an increasingly stimulating part in pedagogy. How would they compare? I have tried to imagine a clutch of prize Fellows from All Souls up against a set of Harvard Junior Fellows and young *agrégés* from the legendary Rue d'Ulm in Paris. How would logicians from Warsaw and Princeton prevail against those of Tübingen or Tartu? It is an entrancing game. My intuition is that in disciplines founded on the classics an Anglo-Scottish contingent from one of those austere Edinburgh academies and one from Pisa would head the table. In political theory, Harvard and LSE might be hard to beat. Who would surpass Chicago in econometrics or Stanford in the crucial interactions between law, sociology, and the natural sciences? In respect of foreign languages and a truly cosmopolitan literacy, certain east European centers, such as Prague and Budapest would most probably rank higher than their more privileged western rivals. A certain parochialism handicaps all but the very peaks of American education.

Overall, my personal experience and recollections amount to a rough and ready finding, obviously subjective. I have never had more demanding, more original students than those in my evening classes at New York University. The multiracial mix around the table, of women and men from the most diverse social backgrounds, of both young and old, of the retired and of those in various professions, made for an implosive cast. The joy of discovery—"Dostoevsky is simply wonderful!"—of intellectual and emotional surprise, the resistance to the merely official and magisterial, the raw vehemence of debate, illustrated the best of the American story. I would pitch some of these students and auditors against any elite. Even that which made a doctoral seminar at Stanford and certain tutorials at Cambridge occasions on which I learned far more than I could aspire to teach. Even when compared with my more or less continuous seminar in comparative literature and intellectual history over a quarter of a century at the University of Geneva or an unforgettable audience in Girona. But these are provisional impressions, inaccessible to quantified analysis. Remembrance is never more than a flash-bulb.

To speak of French education is to touch centrally on deep structures in French history and society. It is, in its post-eighteenth-century format, to consider a bureaucratic unison, a hierarchical meritocracy rivaled only by that of imperial China. One often has the impression that during the Third Republic, also known as the *République des professeurs,* one half of France was more or less perpetually engaged in teaching and examining the other half. Academic performance has been, still is, though to a diminishing extent, a matter of public interest and notice. Exam results are published. At my time, tremulous parents and their children crowded a dirty Paris street in order to see the posters which announced the results of the *baccalauréat*. Annually, the press featured reports of those who fainted, either in relief or desolation. The exact ranking of those who pass the *agrégation* are still made public. Glory can hinge on a fraction of a point. But should this not be so in a competitive trial which has placed Bergson or Sartre or Raymond Aron first and Simone de Beauvoir only second (those who failed, sometimes repeatedly, constitute a galaxy of their own) The quality press publishes the topics set for candidates at the *baccalauréat*. These in turn are debated by pundits. The role of the *philosophes* and publicists during the Enlightenment and French Revolution was vital. Napoleon determined to make of French schooling and scientific-technological research an instrument of controlling power and prestige. After the defeat of 1870–71, France was obsessed with the will to match German pedagogic rigor in secondary and higher instruction. The proliferation of a politicized intelligentsia around the Dreyfus Affair—street battles were waged around the Sorbonne—together with the tumults and polemics of 1968, reached deep into the theory and practice of education. They made of the classroom and university auditorium a disputed matrix of French national identity. No less than major politicians, themselves usually highly literate, no less than writers or eminent entrepreneurs, it has been the guru, the inspired teacher (Alain), the charismatic lecturer at the Collège de France (Barthes, Foucault) who has been a focus of national interest. Where else does a government decorate teachers with *palmes académiques* or name streets not only for poets and field marshals but for pioneering orientalists, scholastic logicians and pure mathematicians? A walk through the Latin Quarter of Paris is a tour of the history of the mind. With every justification, therefore, the French language has imported and naturalized the Chinese rubric "mandarin."

Schooling in France has been characterized by its emphasis on the language. It is the genius of the French language, deemed to excel all others in precision, clarity, and euphonic elegance, which is to be impressed on the pupil from primary school upward. The child is to grasp the instrumental primacy of the language in defining and sustaining the destiny of *la nation*. This credo carries with it a charge, both explicit and internalized, of rhetoric, a trust in eloquence, a reverence for written and oral style. "Style is man." More than once—de Gaulle provides an example—it is high rhetoric which has masked reality and kept disaster at bay. From an early age, the French schoolchild is drilled in the arts of verbal presentation, the *composition*. He studies and imitates the lexical, grammatical treasure trove of the national classics (*explication de texte,* also *pastiche,* the young Marcel Proust's favorite exercise). First and foremost, he or she is made to learn by heart, to memorize passages of steadily increasing length and density. First La Fontaine, later Valéry. Memorization is key. It wakes and nurtures the muscles of attention—attention and concentration being, as Malebranche teaches, the "natural piety" of the spirit. It initiates a community of shared reference, a shorthand of recognized inheritance. It stores within us resources of feeling which can neither be censored nor pillaged. Accurate, apposite quotation, mimetic pride in the legacy of great texts, rhetorical ornamentation of all aspects of civic life, establish a direct continuity between school and nation. *Lycées* bear the names of eminent writers and thinkers. Recent social transformations and globalization have only partially eroded this defining axis.

A further distinctive feature of traditional French schooling is that of the teaching of philosophy already at the secondary school level. Before his *baccalauréat,* the student was introduced to classics of philosophic argument and controversy. He was acquainted, although in preliminary fashion, with metaphysical notions in Plato and Descartes, with aspects of Comte's positivism and, perhaps, of modern existentialism. Distinguished instructors chose to teach in these "terminal" classes rather than in the university. Questions posed in public examinations, in the *concours* for admission to the *École Normale* might draw on Rousseau and Hegel no less than on Bergson or Sartre. Is there any other educational system which asks teenagers to discuss whether "Ethics can be termed knowledge" or "Are all proofs of existence circular"? As the titular incarnation of this corpus of canonical thought and literature, even in a provincial or ill-equipped *lycée,* a teacher benefited from an esteem, from conventions of civic respect comparable only to those which he enjoyed in pre-1914 Germany and the Austro-Hungarian Empire. It was a privilege not lightly to be exercised to have *Monsieur* or *Madame le Professeur* as a guest in one's home. Bergson, Sartre, Simone Weil taught the young. As did Mallarmé.

How much of this is left? What inroads have been made on ever-more-urgent critiques of a backward-looking classicism, of the rhetorical bombast, of the immature sophistries and high gossip generated by certain ideals in traditional French upbringing? France's relative decline in the sciences—not in pure mathematics and certain branches of engineering—may reflect a schooling saturated by humanistic, even archaic values. Do the arts of memory stifle spontaneity, do they discourage the innovations, the heresies crucial to progress in science? Immersion in its iconic language has placed French intellectual life on the defensive. The Anglo-American tide is reaching deep inland. French intellectual life is on the defensive. The Anglo-American tide is reaching deep inland. French culture is finding it difficult to cope. Even in the fine arts. Are the abstractions and conformities inherent in the French academic mandarinate atrophying? I owe to my *lycée* teachers so very much of what has made my life worth living. But it may be that bumbling Mr. Chips was a more useful guide to humane survival than Valéry's *Monsieur Teste*.

The changes in secondary and higher education in the United Kingdom over these past decades have been momentous and confused. The plans for reform put forward by official commissions, by educational think-tanks of every political tint, have piled up almost absurdly. Reorganizations have been imposed and countermanded, requirements and syllabi tinkered with. Traditional icons have all but disappeared. The overall tide has been the of leveling downward in an attempt, largely political, to amend generations, perhaps centuries, of social injustice. A few inherited elements subsist. They include an insistence on sport which was initially buttressed by imperial and Victorian identifications with ancient Sparta, Athens, and Rome. Where French children tend to limp home under their book bags, their British counterparts are toiling on the playing fields. A handful of elite public schools such as Westminster and Winchester (where "public" means "private") continue instruction in the classical languages to a considerable standard of proficiency. In these somewhat austere citadels, there is still a hierarchy of student self-government, rule by "prefects," unlike that in any other education system. But changes have been at once fundamental and chaotic. A structure of "grammar schools" dating back to Tudor times—the one at Stratford-upon-Avon taught Ovid to a promising lad—has been dismantled. What were called "direct-grant schools," often outstanding, were done away with in the name of egalitarian aspirations (though they are now being reclaimed under other names). New universities have mushroomed, too many of them consigned to mediocrity and vocational training. There are degrees in cooking, beauty care and the marketing of aquatic leisure. Technological, polytechnical, junior forms of collegiate training cluster uneasily on the outer edge of genuine university curricula and research. Decisively, the number of British students in one or another branch of tertiary education has multiplied exponentially. It had been alarmingly low. So has the number of young women and of entrants from ethnic minorities. Immigration, the needs of the inner cities, and the welcome extended to overseas students—be it for ill-disguised budgetary motives—have radically altered the entire educational scene. The dialectic is difficult to untangle. If there is a cultural masochism which has impelled Britain to dumb down many of its most enviable achievements, in the media, in the book world, there is also a genuine ache for justice, for the opening of doors of opportunity and advancement too long closed. What is certain is that a Jowett or a Matthew Arnold would struggle to grasp the current picture.

Yet the gap remains. There are distinguished departments, faculties, laboratories outside Oxford, Cambridge, London or Bristol. In some localities "sixth-form colleges" sparkle (the final years of British secondary schooling rival the standards of most American undergraduate education). A number of urban "academies" with more or less open admission have performed admirably in tables of comparative national merit. A pride of girls' schools must rank among the best in the world. Across the board, however, the gap widens—and results are dismal. Too often in England, the adolescent school-leaver, bored out of his fallow mind, barely musters the rudimentary literacies and numeracies demanded by modern life and employment. Her or his reading skills are estimated to be those of an eleven-year-old. Mathematics, of even an elementary standard, are a terra incognita. Ignorance of history, of geography, of a foreign language is monumental. The system is generating a teeming underclass of semiliterates whose vocabulary and command of grammar reduce both feelings and ambitions to bleak vulgarity. Report follows on report, parliamentary and public debate is interminable. Statistics swarm like angry gnats. Meanwhile covert modes of selection multiply and middle-class parents go to crazy lengths—plunging into debt, moving house, pretending to religious affiliations—in order to secure quality schooling for their offspring. Despite recriminations and seasonal threats by Labour governments, the top schools (in which, fortunately, the ancient delights of physical bullying have waned) conserve and augment their privileged clientele. Bursaries and tutorial support for the less fortunate do help; but barriers are still in place.

Arcadia, also, is under pressure. Increasingly—I will revert to this—the tradition, perhaps unique to the United Kingdom, of early, intense specialization embodied in A-level teaching and exams is proving inappropriate to the actual world. Training in depth covered three or, at most, four subjects, often interrelated. Compared to the *baccalauréat* or the *Matura* with their general spectrum, A-levels are damagingly narrow. The elevated context of literacy, familial and social, in which the young Etonian grew up may have made possible extreme specialization at the secondary level. This privileged background can no longer be assumed. Even the better universities are having to cope with an alarming dearth of general knowledge and intellectual skills. The palmy days in which sixth-form disciplines in classics, history, foreign languages, literature or mathematics sufficed to equip students for higher education and the professions are largely over. Hence the recalcitrant moves toward an international *baccalauréat,* toward a curriculum in which a thirteen-year-old cannot cheerily abandon any further contact with mathematics or the sciences. (Who is to teach the new range? Hence also the need to introduce, even at Oxbridge, introductory and survey courses on the American model.) Elite universities are under grim financial stress. How long will they sustain the vital luxuries of face-to-face tutorials, of the weekly essay individually set and judged? Yet it is these which gave to the finest of British pedagogy its stylish excellence.

Brilliance is not licensed to subvert a robust philistinism. In

England—less so in Scotland—"cleverness," too manifest an intellectual passion, "brainy" ambition and those mandarin values pervasive in France, have long been distrusted. They are chastised both in school and the body politic. "Intellectual" comes close to being a term of reproach or derision. "Thinker" is not an epithet at home in the language. The splendors of English literature, of the sciences since Roger Bacon, of moments in British philosophical discourse, have not effaced this entrenched dismissal. A recent poll asking for a list of those who had mattered most in national consciousness put Darwin in tenth place. Statesmen and athletes headed the roll. It is today's pop stars who crowd the guest list at 10 Downing Street. The yield, however, is far from being altogether negative. It is precisely this philistinism, this distaste for any *odium theologicum* (has Britain produced any theologians of the first order besides Duns Scotus and Henry Newman?), it is just this distrust of the abstract and the ideological which have afforded English history its enviable record of tolerance, of ironic immunity to the intellectually charismatic. Balking at argumentative brio, at cerebral furies and commitment—French *engagement*—the English have preferred an ironizing pragmatism, a saving indifference. Neither fascism nor Leninist-Stalinism could rouse the emotions of any but a handful. Neither Pascal nor Nietzsche, neither Kierkegaard nor Marx stand high in the English pantheon. What counts is the colorless, low-key tolerance, and calm good sense exemplified by Locke. What is needed is a thorough anatomy of the relations between English education and this therapeutic anti-intellectualism. And, perhaps, a subdued celebration thereof.

Locke's hopeful sobriety informed the ideals of the American constitution and the instauration of American political institutions. But history soon became overwhelming in its continental dimensions and local particularities. The diverse school systems which have proliferated in the United States, the kaleidoscope of vocational, technical, and higher education are so various as to render irresponsible any generalizations or attempted summary. Immensely complex pressures such as race and religion intervene. Methods and standards differ not only from state to state, but within state boundaries. School districts have their own history and purpose. States such as Pennsylvania and Ohio are home to several hundred colleges, ranging from denominational campuses serving a congregation of the faithful to outsized state universities in which tens of thousands are enrolled. Land-grant colleges and universities border on those founded by the largesse of a single patron (Stanford, Duke, Pepperdine). No other society offers a comparable gamut. I have been a student at the University of Chicago and at Harvard; a guest professor at Princeton, Yale, Stanford, and Santa Barbara. Even this experience is only minimalist.

It is a banality to note the deluge of subliteracy which has engulfed much of American secondary schooling. Evidence is somewhat surreal. The most proverbial of scriptural allusions, of references to world classics go unrecognized. Seminal dates, even in American history, draw a blank. Some eighty percent of high school graduates could not tell whether Ireland lies to the east or the west of Great Britain. Undergraduates, even at reputable colleges or universities cannot assign Aquinas, Galileo, or Pasteur to their appropriate century. An understanding of sentences with dependent clauses is dwindling, as is the available vocabulary. For a growing majority, even the elements of calculus are an arcane mystery. The catalog of emptiness runs on. The statistics of school dropouts, of the near-illiterate worsen from decade to decade. Ideological insinuations add to the dilemmas of what has been called, by American observers, "our idiocracy." There is the pap and censorship of "political correctness"; the blackmail of religious conservatism, even fundamentalism, in the conservative heartlands, but also in "middle America." Irony, skeptical inquiry are unpatriotic. Attempts to muzzle the theory of evolution are only the most notorious example. Yet at the very top, American graduate training is incomparable. It leads the planet in the pure and applied sciences, in business studies. America is the powerhouse of international scientific publications, of medical research, of information theory and technology. Microsoft and Google span the Earth. It is to the great American libraries and archives that the European scholar must resort. The tawdry violence and pedagogic misery of an inner-city high school will neighbor on a college campus or university, or on a hub of research that is the envy of the world.

Such antitheses arise from a fundamental contradiction already visible to de Tocqueville. The republic is founded on the promise of equal opportunity, of constant melioration. America is always tomorrow. It proclaims the "pursuit of happiness" in an egalitarian community never dreamt of by other societies. The contract with hope is not directed toward disinterested knowledge, particularly knowledge of the past, but to the realization of "Californias" to come. Today, more than ever before, the goal of schooling is that of a unifying patriotism, of national pride, and integration under an American deity. Out of *pluribus unum*. It is not with a recitation from a classic or a multiplication table that the school day begins: it is with a pledge of allegiance to the American flag. Moreover, despite setbacks, despite extensive pockets of economic and social deprivation, despite racial tensions which persist intractably, the success of the American experiment has been such as to justify much of its utopian hubris. What other nation can compare in respect of generosities, material and psychological, in the number of those whom it has provided with a life of unprecedented ease and prosperity? To hundreds of millions in Africa or Asia, an American slum would seem Eden. Education, therefore, is not an end in itself. It is not a training for solitude or for historical crisis. In the United States, it has been the alphabet of a social and political dream. The distance from disenchanted, commemorative Europe is formidable. My son, who occupies a significant posting in the theory and politics of American education, affirms that

"Europe preserves form, America has content." This must be an erroneous shibboleth. But is it?

The crux is that these sunlit ideals run counter to the grain of human reality. Intellectually, women and men are no less diversely endowed than they are physically. Assisted improvement can achieve much, but its limits are not boundlessly elastic. A terrible unfairness separates the gifted from the common. The nightmare would be, most markedly in America, if it did turn out that this unfairness has ethnic correlations. That it has genetic components. Who promised the human species that biological realities would accord with, would empower, decency? Social justice is no accomplice to excellence. It levels downward. It is to America's honor that it seeks to refute these bents in nature, that it strives to amend—though often somewhat hypocritically—these constants of injustice in the mortal condition. The price paid is steep. It is not only that political mediocrity, corruption, and illiterate populism flourish. It is that intellectual eminence is so often marginalized, that the love of the language withers under the steamroller of mass-media infantilism. Popular democracy and the life of the mind are essentially at odds, precisely as Plato and de Tocqueville foresaw. Intellectual obsession is a cancer of aloneness, alien to, profoundly suspect within the gregarious clamor of the American climate.

Perhaps the question to be asked is this: What would be a core literacy adequate to the spiritual and practical needs of men and women on a multinational, increasingly intermeshed planet?

In the West, the notion of "literacy" is inseparable from the growth of monasticism and church schools after the decay of the Roman Empire. To be "literate" signified the ability to read Scripture, to form letters on the page. This capacity, often rudimentary, defined the cleric and the clerk, these two designations being closely related. Some familiarity with Latin, though often in hybrid and transitional forms and, only very rarely, some access to classical Greek, via Byzantium or Islam, attached to ecclesiastical, legal, bureaucratic, and diplomatic dignities. This literate elite, these men of letters (there were a few exceptional women among them) assured, in the most pragmatic sense, the fragmentary preservation and transmission of ancient civilization, a transmission mitigated, amended by Christian revelation. Literacy thus defined a "clerisy" and those ideological and political power relations which made possible the governance of church and state. It is from this legacy, set out incomparably in Dante's tracts on the vulgate and on literary education, that modern Western concepts of literacy and of its usages—where "modern" simply means post-medieval—derive.

This inheritance carried with it a blurring of the term "literacy." It took on at least two principal significations. At its more elevated level, literacy came to stand for the shared *communitas,* for the shared code of reference of the learned. It pointed to their ownership of the material means of reading and writing. It came to underwrite, itself a suggestive term, the great age of the private library from Erasmus and Montaigne to the mid-twentieth century. It comprised the producers and consumers of literature—note the source and content of that word—the lawmakers and divines, the scientists both natural and philosophical, the political thinkers and historians, the metaphysicians and the poets. St. Jerome at his desk is iconic of that commonwealth of grammar. Belles lettres and "bookmen," "readers" in the academic hierarchy (this rubric persists in British higher education to this day) correspondents in public and private affairs across the European *civilitas,* women and men who could "write letters," are categories which illustrate the breadth and centrality of the word "literacy." Very gradually, by reluctant osmosis, high culture and communicative techniques seeped downward. It influenced, in some measure, the rudimentary, often minimal capacities to read and write at all. Libraries became public, schooling expanded. In the wake of the Enlightenment, of the French and industrial revolutions, of Victorian didactic, social meliorism—consider the key functions of literacy in John Stuart Mill, in Matthew Arnold—and early models of the welfare state, literacy spread to the population at large. the role of printing and of printed mater, such as the cheap press, is both essential and conspicuous. But let us be careful. Even in this second, wider sense, literacy often was and indeed remains marginal. For generations, instruction remained elementary. The vast majority of the agricultural and laboring classes, of women in domestic or menial employment, of early school-leavers, were literate in only the most superficial and restricted sense. At best, they could make out basic texts. Their writing skills were virtually inert. What books could they read, let alone own? Social historians continue to excavate this opaque condition. The indices are graphic. More than one third of French conscripts in 1914–18 had to be trained in remedial reading of a rough-and-ready kind. I have already alluded to a comparable backwardness among British school-leavers. In the United States, purveyors of advertisements and the mass media aim, whereever feasible, to avoid words of more than two syllables and any subjunctives. Dependent clauses are all but effaced. The question of whether the majority of those who purchase medication are able to decipher the labels and instructions has reached critical urgency. In the so-called "third world," in much of Asia, Africa, Latin America, but also in rural regions of Mediterranean Europe, literacy remains sporadic. The educational potential of television is manifest. So far, however, blessings are ambiguous. The picture lords it over the caption. There have been efficacious impositions of mass literacy from above in Turkey, in the Soviet Union, and in large parts of China. These are the direct consequences of dictatorial political will. Dictators can dictate. Mass-market democracy is more lenient. As a superstar in the heavens of British sport and fashion, role model to millions, asked: "And why should I be into books?"

In tandem with the uneven deployment of literacy came the prodigious development of the sciences, theoretical and applied, pure and technological. This development dates back to Babylonian astronomy, to Pythagoras and to Plato's celebration of geometry. We have seen how Needham explored its archaic Chinese origins. But the definitive breakthrough can be ascribed to Galileo's postulate that the language of nature, of reality in motion, when these are grasped and ordered by human reason, is that of mathematics. It was the exponential enrichment of mathematical tools and concepts which fueled the history of cosmology and physics from Galileo and Kepler to Newton and Einstein. Mathematical statistics inform the Darwinian theory of evolution and molecular biology. No systematic meteorology or genetics, no experimental psychology or behavioral science without algebraic and topological instruments. Even disciplines long regarded as innocent of mathematics, such as linguistics, social theory, and anthropology became increasingly dependent on algebraic algorithms. Such awkward labels as "econometrics" or "cliometrics" tell of this ubiquity. The worlds of the computer and of information theory, of artificial intelligence and the Web are those of mathematics.

Inevitably, the necessary levels of numeracy rose with every generation. First-year undergraduates are now required to familiarize themselves with algebraic manipulations which would have disconcerted Gauss or Hardy. Serious students of economics, of actuarial or demographic patterns, operate with theorems reserved, not long ago, to the domain of pure mathematics. On their computers schoolchildren play with the crystalline structures of fractals. Observing the imperialism of the mathematical in the sciences, in technology, in philosophic logic and the mechanization of our daily lives, one has the impression of an internalized dynamics, of a drive for acquisition like no other. As Galileo and Descartes professed, a body of knowledge, a gathering of data and insight only ripens to being a science, to being a coherent discipline when it can to a greater or lesser degree be mathematicized.

One consequence has been the "two cultures" debate. It seems to me that in all the ill-tempered polemics which C. P. Snow initiated, an absolutely crucial point has been overlooked. The fundamental difference between the humanities and the sciences is the arrow of time. Virtually by definition, the sciences and technology move forward. Tomorrow is richer, more encompassing than today. New knowledge, new theoretical possibilities will be available next Monday. Even a routine scientist or engineer is working on an upward escalator if and when he or she participates in a qualified team or laboratory (science is now primarily teamwork). In the greater part of his enterprise the Western humanist looks ever backward. He studies, he teaches, he comments on the philosophies, the literatures, the music, the fine arts, and the history of the past. He celebrates the Bach anniversaries or the Mozart year. He is housed in the archives, in the monumental, in the museum. In the opera houses, symphony halls or chamber-music recitals, some ninety percent of programing draws on the classics. The humanities strive to quicken into renewed life remembrance of things past. Logically, inductively there is absolutely no reason why a new Shakespeare or Michelangelo or Beethoven should not appear on the scene tomorrow morning; why the next Goethe should not be drafting his unprecedented *Faust* in the highrise apartment building next door. But how many of us, whatever our passions for modern, experimental art, truly believe in such epiphany? Resist, if you can, the seductions of facile pathos, of sunset in the Spenglerian vein; dismiss Valéry's warning as to the mortality of our civilization; involve yourself receptively with conceptual art, with electronic and aleatory music, with postmodern writing. Still the intuition gnaws: The humanities and arts in the West are virtuosities of twilight and recollection.

The reasons for this elude confident diagnosis. The phenomenon itself could be optical illusion. Renaissance theorists told of incipient decline. But if there is sunset, it may point toward the eventuality that "tiredness" is a psychic and collective truth as well as a physiological fact. An enormity of past history, in both senses of the word, weighs on Europe and on all that is archival in the American Eden. In thought, in the arts, precedent can both inspire and lame. Bent over a blank page, Keats puzzles how he can inscribe the word "tragedy" when Sophocles and Shakespeare are looking over his shoulder. Note the cunning of recuperation in so many of our twentieth-century masters. Joyce enlists Homer, Picasso overtly anthologizes the unfolding of Western art from the cave paintings to Velasquez and Manet, Stravinsky plays metamorphic changes on Renaissance, Baroque and eighteenth-century templates. Eliot's "The Waste Land," Pound's *Cantos* are a terminal, almost frantic rush to catalog the past before the museum shuts down. Historians estimate at anywhere between seventy and one hundred million the number of those done to death by war, famine, deportation, forced labor and outright genocide between August 1914 and May 1945 in Europe and the European portions of Russia. Whatever their global extension, both world wars were European civil wars. Current material recovery is, in many respects, trompe-l'oeil, an electric shock setting a dead limb in motion. The century of massacres (it persists), the Shoah, may have altered the very status of individual death. It is this status which is elemental in past art, literature, and metaphysics, which instilled in Western consciousness a hunger for transcendence. As the *Commedia* teaches, the humanities, in the deepest, most creative sense, aim to "eternalize" man—*come l'uom s'eterna*. Can we still credit this purpose? Would a return to humanistic performance of the first order be anything less than a miracle?

The question of literacy, of what "literacy" in this twenty-first century should or could signify, now comports a new, in many respects decisive, factor. I feel tempted to call it "a third culture." It is that of the electronic, computational revolution as it has flowered out of the algorithms of encoding and code-breaking of the Second World War. For some eighty years after Gutenberg, manuscripts continued to be produced and esteemed. The revolution which has generated the modern computer, the Internet, the global web, the planetary marketing of information via satellites (can knowledge be *owned*?), artificial intelligence, and the theoretically unlimited means of storage and retrieval in memory banks and search mechanisms (Google), is of incalculable power and consequence. "Technique," as Hegel and Heidegger used the term, is an insufficient concept. The computer world together with the accelerating rate of its development and distribution, also to the home and primary schools, is one in which fundamental constants such as knowledge, information, communication, psychological and social control, indeed our understanding of the human brain and nervous system ("wiring") are being radically altered and revalued. The robot is stealing nearer to the acts of thought. The conjecture advanced by cosmologists and neurophysiologists whereby our universe and the place of the human cortex within it can best be imaged as computer-designed, as generated by synapses in a "web of webs," has a speculative force beyond science fiction.

Day by day, computer literacy is becoming the *rite de passage* into the adolescent and adult spheres. In the industrialized West, computer training begins almost in infancy and an ever-increasing competence is required for access to higher education. The computer is the indispenable tool in business and finance, in government and the organization of the media and of medicine, in every facet of design and the craft of war. Its advance into private life, into every cranny of leisure, looks to be irresistible. No previous artifact or invention, certainly since man's domestication of fire, will have exercised the shaping impact on everyday human pursuits brought about by the PC and the laptop, by mobile texting and the

Internet. The electronic screen has become the mirror for man. Already it is likely that those communities and individuals (myself among them) incapable of mastering the processor and the "mouse," the search mechanisms and "surfing" will be relegated to a new underclass, to being helots of oblivion. Arrestingly, moreover, this "third culture" partakes of both the humanities and the sciences. Its roots lie in mathematical logic and electro-magnetic equations. But its informational content, its iconography, and referential reach encompass every semiotic construct, every linguistic application whether in literature, history, the study of the fine arts or formal logic. Unquestionably, this pervasiveness will, over time, have its "feedback," inflecting patterns of human thought and habits of perception.

The hope of preserving or resuscitating humanistic literacy in any traditional mode seems to me illusory. That literacy, that dominion of the classical belonged to an elite. As I have noted, the democratization of schooling and political society runs counter to the Platonic ideals aimed for in the class divisions and power relations in education throughout the *ancien régime* or Victorian and Edwardian Britain. Receptivity to higher culture is far from natural or universal. It can be nurtured and multiplied, but only to a limited extent. The study of Greek irregular verbs or of Horace's metrics will always have engaged the few. In a more general, though not altogether evident sense, the ability to take in complex arguments, to respond to a Platonic dialogue, to a tractate by Spinoza, a treatise by Kant or a Shakespearean sonnet characterizes a minority. This is true as well of the arts and of classical and modern music. A fog of political hypocrisy and pedagogic cant shrouds this entire issue. "Political correctness," penitential submission to the rights of populism, make it virtually ilicit to confront the deeplying barriers which may separate the majority of men and women from access to the high places, to Yeats's "monuments of unageing intellect."

The inability of high culture to defend its corner effectively, what has been called "the treason of the clerics," stems from a grim if often repressed insight. Twentieth-century barbarism burst from within the heartland of European civilization. It flourished in the very locale of esthetic and philosophic merit. The death camps were built neither in the Gobi Desert nor in Equatorial Africa. And when barbarism challenged, the humanities, the arts, much of philosophic inquiry proved impotent. What is worse, culture collaborated decoratively with despotism and massacre. There was many a lover of fine arts and classical music among the butchers, many a teacher of great literature among the sycophants. The mere designation *literae humaniores* now rings hollow.

After more than fifty years of trying to read great literature and philosophic texts with my students, I am haunted by a possibility. I call it the "Cordelia paradox." As one comes home from reading and re-reading acts three, four and five of *King Lear,* from watching a performance, from attempting, however inadequately, to grasp and evaluate these experiences, the cry in the text, on the stage possesses our consciousness. It fills our being. The fiction overwhelms what Freud called the "reality principle." The cry of tortured Lear, the torment of Gloucester and Cordelia blot out the world. We do not hear the cry in the street. Or if we do hear it, we do not listen to it, let alone hurry to give help. Far from humanizing our reflexes, as Aristotle or Matthew Arnold would have it, the major fictions, the masterpieces of art, the spellbinding melodies inhibit our *answerability*—a key word—to immediate human need, suffering and injustice. In some numbing way, they can dehumanize. Whether it is feasible to steep oneself in, to internalize and echo the agony of Lear so as to strengthen, to render more concrete our moral and civic resources, is a question to which I have no answer. Tolstoy ruled that it could not be done.

Underlying the crisis in the humanities, be it political, social or psychological, is that erosion of organized religion which I adduced at the outset. Traditional literacy and the culture and schooling which it engendered were indeed moored to theological suppositions and values. As our civilization drifts, literacy is cast loose. As so-called "post-modernism" clarions, "anything goes." This does not mean that we will cease from producing and reading books, some of them worthwhile, from visiting museums or building concert halls. Of course we will. Audiences may widen. Much can be read on the Internet or appreciated inholographic reproductions. Why not download the *Missa solemnis*? Pessimism has its snobbery. What it does mean is that such joys, and the efforts they necessarily entail, will compete, on a common scale of prestige and economic support, with mass entertainment of the most brutal and deafening kind, with sport (the real theodicy is that of the soccer shoot-out). The serious bookstore will compete, on absurdly uneven terms, with the pornography emporium next door. More and more sometime mandarins and artists will strive for stardom in the mass media. The harsh benedictions of privacy and of silence, of unpopularity on which serious thought and original creation so often depend, will be increasingly difficult to come by. Democracy is wary of aloneness. Even to Plato, to Goethe or Proust, the criteria of the supermarket may come to apply that cynical, trivializing gallicism: *ce n'est que de la littérature.*

"What then shall we do?" as Lenin famously asked.

As I said, the array of education acts, of charters for reform, of federal hearings on the crises in our schools are legion. What noble trees have been pulped to supply this never-ending stream of officious trash!

Certain remedies lie to hand. Even the most efficient and devoted of school teachers are being systematically humiliated and prevented from doing their proper job by mountains of legalistic paperwork and coercive red tape. They are poorly remunerated and condescended to. The consequence has been an automatism of self-destruction. It is too often the least academically inspired who drift into secondary teaching, thus transmitting their own saddened mediocrity to generations of bored pupils. I need hardly cite the erosion of elementary discipline and courtesy in the classroom, an erosion precipitated by physical violence, parental threats, and legalistic interference. It is a truism, long admitted, that neither British A-levels nor the American high-school curriculum, set in a matrix in which the basketball coach earns more than the math teacher, equips one for the modern world. Yet time after time, authentic reform, the adoption in the United Kingdom of an international *baccalauréat* to remedy the absurd contraction of vital skills, to allow a grounding in both the humanities and the sciences have been shelved by special interests and an establishment frightened by innovation. Who can number the attempts to enforce in American schooling an attainment of genuine writing skills or some competence in foreign languages and numeracy? Such aims are wholly in reach of good sense and political will (Stalinism organized formidable levels of literacy, of arithmetic capacities, of the learning of languages by elevating teachers' salaries and social status). None of this requires witchcraft.

If standards are to be reaffirmed, populist claims will have to yield to an order of merit in which genuine excellence can be distinguished from the mushroom growth of parasitic forms. All that is lacking is political nerve which will expose and defy that disdain for intellectual life, that distrust of eminence characteristic of mass consumption in late capitalism. (One recalls the brief but intoxicating summons to education and intellectual adventure which lit the United States in the wake of the Soviet launching of space travel.) Again: we must acknowledge that human talents, the means for concentrated mental effort are unevenly distributed.

That not every man and woman can ingest (Ben Jonson's telling idiom) Kant on synthetic a priori or a nonlinear equation. "Elite" means something very simple: it signifies that some things are finer than others, that no one is admitted to a physics department without mathematical competence, that Bob Dylan, entrancing as are his gifts, does not equal Keats. The Last Judgment will, I suspect, be a *concours* run by French examiners.

But urgent and far-reaching as these issues are, they do not go to the heart of the matter. Which is that of a fundamental literacy, of a conceptual core for the women and men of today and tomorrow ("core curriculum" is a useful shorthand). By "literacy" I mean the ability to engage with, to respond to, what is most challenging and creative in our societies. To experience and contribute to the energies of informed debate. To distinguish the "new which stays news," as Ezra Pound put it, from the tidal waves of ephemeral rubbish, superstition, irrationalism, and commercial exploitation. Can we draft such a central syllabus for both intellect and feeling? Can we sketch a "base" correspondent to the latent strengths of the imagination, a central axis of roused awareness interactive with the demands and fascination of the world?

The provisional suggestions I now put forward will seem utopian, perhaps scandalously so. But there are times of crisis in which only the utopian is realistic.

The eclipse of numeracy throughout our culture, the ignorance among those who regard themselves as educated in mathematical concepts and procedures are at once a cliché and a misery. There is scarcely any constituent in the ways in which our world operates in which mathematical operations do not play a major role. It is not only nature which speaks mathematics, it is modern life. Yet the relevant elements are to a vast majority of us a rebarbative mystery or a dim recollection of school classes wretchedly taught and happily forgotten. Go around the room asking family or friends to define a "mean average."

The loss extends far beyond the pragmatic. The rapacious, territorial, often sadistic mammal that is man has generated a handful of activities, of constructs of consciousness which are nonutilitarian and of transcendent beauty. These "motions of spirit" (Dante) include music, poetry, metaphysics. Their origin remains a consoling enigma. Above all, they comprise pure mathematics. The debate as to whether mathematical abstractions have their validating counterpart in external reality as Plato held, or whether they are autonomous mental "play," axiomatic games of mesmerizing depth and purity developed, as it were, from within, remains unresolved. This debate touches on what is most mysterious in the resources and dreams of the human psyche. What is not in doubt is the sheer beauty, the unfolding elegance, even, at certain points, the wit of the mathematical enterprise. To have encountered Euclid, as Edna St. Vincent Millay expressed it, is to have "looked on beauty bare." It is indeed in mathematics that Keats's somewhat rhetorical equivalence between truth and beauty has its fulfillment. This "beauty" however has an exact, substantive meaning all but inaccessible to the non-numerate. To all those who cannot take in what Leibniz intended when he opined that when "He sings to himself, God sings algebra."

The prevalent view is that beyond rudimentary rote, mathematics can be imparted only to the specially gifted. The grim fact is that so much of the teaching is in the hands of the defeated, of those whose own attainments were wanting. Thus the feedback is negative and the spiral downward. Undoubtedly, there are innate, perhaps resistant differences between aptitudes to numeracy. But these have been grossly exaggerated. Hence my conviction that even advanced mathematical concepts can be made imaginatively compelling and demonstrable when they are presented *historically*. What must be set out is the intellectual, also social, history which lies behind them and which led to solutions or nonsolutions—the latter being perhaps the most fascinating and instructive category. It is via these great voyages and adventures of the human mind, so often charged with personal rivalries, passions and frustrations—the argosy founders or gets trapped in the ice of the insoluble—that we nonmathematicians can look into a sovereign and decisive realm. Let me cite two examples.

During millennia and in numerous civilizations, mathematical postulates and proofs have been assumed to be what is most certain, most unimpugnable in human thought. Plato, Descartes, Spinoza associated their certitude with the necessary existence of the divine. The axiomatic was the very emblem of eternity and perfection. Some doubts began to emerge in the nineteenth century as paradoxes arose from non-Euclidean geometries. On October 7, 1930, in Kant's city of Königsberg, a very young, unknown mathematical logician took what his citation at Harvard many years later described as the greatest step in human thought since Descartes. Kurt Gödel proved that in every consistent formal system there exist propositions which are undecidable. For the system to cohere, there will always have to be one or more rule or proposition imported, as it were, from outside its axiomatic totality. When Gödel's proof came to be understood and applied, the foundations of mathematics, which are in turn those of science as a whole, were seen to have been irremediably fractured. The new worlds would be those of indeterminacy. Einstein, who revered Gödel, could, on emotional grounds, never come to terms with this cataclysm. Its impact, moreover, extended far beyond mathematics, physics, and logic. It put in radical question what had long been taken to be the limitless, certifiable progress of calculable rationality. It would allow Roger Penrose to refute all seductive analogies between computers and the human cortex. This inspired critique culminates in the finding that "thanks to Gödel's theorem, the mind always has the last word." Even if, especially where, that word is one of uncertainty. An awesome freedom has been regained. One can hardly fathom what would have been Galileo's or Spinoza's reaction.

My second example draws on prime numbers. These are the building blocks of our universe ("only God," said one great mathematician, "could have invented prime numbers"). Any alert child can begin to manipulate their magic. Developed in the 1860s by Bernhard Riemann, the Riemann Hypothesis concerns the distribution of primes—we know their number to be infinite—and their relation to zero. The hypothesis is that this distribution can be mapped along a "ley line," allowing one to predict where the next prime number will turn up. A pride of mathematicians, many of towering stature, set out to prove Riemann's intuitively persuasive supposition. Their labors animated not only concentrated genius but personal rivalries of the fiercest kind. Again and again, proof has seemed tantalizingly close. Again and again, a flaw has been detected in the chain of demonstration. Proponents have sometimes suffered mental collapse and even suicide. As the most recent historian of this enthralling saga puts it (he is himself an eminent pure mathematician): "Despite the best efforts of the greatest mathematical minds to explain the modulation and transformation of this mystical music, the primes remain an unanswered riddle. We still await the person whose name will live forever as the mathematician who made the primes sing."

Locate this quest within its intellectual, historical, social and even ideological fabric, rouse the child and the student to the inexhaustible fun and provocation of the unsolved, and you will have flung open doors on "seas of thought" deeper, more richly stocked than any on the globe.

The persistent interleaving of mathematical and musical terms and concepts, the assertion that "primes have music in them" are no accident. From Pythagoras onward, it has been understood that the relations between music and number theory are organic. The immensely influential conceit of the "music of the spheres" buttressed Kepler's conviction that the elliptical functions which govern planetary motions are of a musical order, that the rubric *harmonia mundi* has a perfectly empirical and demonstrable sense. Pythagoras, Kepler, Leibniz would have rejoiced in the designation as "background noise" of those radio waves which are now regarded as the vestiges and validation of the Big Bang which triggered our universe into being. Examine a Bach canon or a Boulez score and their close affinities with algebraic codes and patterns become visible.

Numerous ethnic communities and traditions do not manifest what could justly be entitled "literature." No society on earth, however "primitive," however underprivileged economically or ecologically, exists without music. Musical notation, whether formally written down or not, is like that of arithmetic, a universal language far beyond the aspirations of any conceivable Esperanto. A hit tune will resound simultaneously in the backyards of Patagonia and the bars of Vladivostok. Electronic transmission, downloading, every form of disc have boundlessly multiplied this planetary ubiquity. The languages of music need no translators (nor do those of calculus). Yet as obvious as is the role of music in individual and collective existence—how many of us would want to live without it?—so many riddles remain. To define music as organized sound is to beg the question. Can the often harmonious, syncopated sounds emitted by birds or by whales be defined as music in the proper sense? Is music singular to the human species? Intuition suggests that musical forms, even complex ones, preceded the evolution of speech. If so, how did they originate? Marxism adduces collective, choral emissions during shared labor. Lévi-Strauss is more cautious: "The invention of melody is the supreme mystery in the sciences of man." Each and every one of us—is there genuine tone-deafness?—will have experienced the power of music to seize upon our emotions, to quicken sorrow or joy, ferocity or tenderness, dynamic anticipation or nostalgia. How does music work inside us, what are its contiguities with our nervous system, with our innards? Why are we indifferent to tunes others find unforgettable? How can it be that identical compositions, such as Beethoven's setting of Schiller's "Ode to Joy," can serve as anthems for totally opposed political and ideological movements? First and foremost, there is the semantic crux. Music and compositions are charged with meaning. But when we seek to articulate this meaning, to paraphrase it verbally, the result is either vaguely metaphoric or of a desperate banality. Only program music is translatable. Music is meaningful in the extreme. For many of us it comes closer than any other human happening to communicating the possible proximity of the transcendent. But strictly considered, *it has no sense.* In essence, its overwhelming force is useless. It is this potent non-utility which exasperated and worried Plato; it is this anarchic "unemployment" which made him restrict music to athletic and military functions in the ideal polis.

Learning to sing or play an instrument within the bounds of one's natural endowments—the most brilliant of living percussionists is stone deaf—is a formidable enhancement of both psychic and social resources. Music can be the therapy of the hurt spirit also, as has long been suspected, in a medical perspective. To understand music is to be confronted with the surprisingly confining limits of language. Only dance, perhaps, can explicate music. Asked to explain a difficult étude, Schumann simply played it a second, then a third time. Now it is precisely this utter presence beyond verbal paraphrase or proof, beyond logical diagnosis, which seems to attach to the "borderline" but immensely significant phenomena of religious belief, of eros and of death. *Pace* Wittgenstein, the limits of language are not those of my world. Nietzsche saw much deeper when he defined music as the *mysterium tremendum* of the unfathomably obvious.

Architecture has been called "frozen music." It has also been described as "geometry in motion." The kinship between music and architecture is celebrated in classical mythology and practice. Music attends the founding of cities. Flutes resound as the Athenians erect the walls of the Piraeus; Thebes arises to the tune of Arion's lyre. As Valéry has it in his Platonic dialogue on architecture, the purpose of the architect is to "redistribute light, endowed with intelligible forms and almost musical perspectives, into the space where mortals move." To those who have been taught to listen, "a façade can sing." In both architecture and music, essential aspects of harmony, proportions, and thematic variation are related. In turn, these aspects are fundamentally geometric and algebraic. Numerical harmonics generate their beauty and their truth. The animate temple, observes Valéry, "is the mathematical image of the girl of Corinth." In a manner far surpassing simile, divine creation is, in creation myths across the planet and in Plato's *Timaeus,* the deed of a supreme architect, of a master builder. (Cross-reference: Ibsen's ironic reprise of this motif.) The compass and the plumb line are the symbols of the cosmic blueprint.

Today we are in one of the stellar periods of architecture in all history. Public and private buildings, bridges of stunning beauty and innovation, are being built all over the globe. The relevant theoretical considerations and techniques extend from geology, material sciences, engineering, and design to higher mathematics. They engage economics and social planning, transport, urbanization, and ecology in its most urgent and embracing horizons. To be initiated into the functions of architecture in contemporary life is to encounter cardinal dilemmas in the state of our cities, of our mobility, of what ideals we may still harbor as to social justice and health care. Having witnessed so much violent destruction, having seen the tragic fragility of our proudest towers, we are now in a fever of construction which, despite etymology, is often anything but edification. It is, furthermore, in today's architecture that we engage with the computer at its most creative. There is architecture before the computer and after. The borderline and transition can be exemplified by the differences between the as yet experimental, tactile mathematics of the Sydney Opera House and the computer-generated, computer-controlled marvels of the Guggenheim Museum in Bilbao or the Jewish Museum in Berlin. In both these cases, design and realization would not have been feasible without high-power holographic modeling and exact computation. "Give the gold medal to the computer," quipped Gehry when describing his Bilbao project. In correlation, electronic music is emitted to "argue," to activate the conceptual spaces in the access to the Tate Modern in London. To be taught to "read" a building is to be made literate in respect of much that is most beautiful and expressive in modernity.

The fourth synapse in our core literacy, in the new *quadrivium,* would be an introduction to molecular biology and genetics. The veritable explosion of these disciplines since the mapping of DNA and its double helix is altering the texture of private and public affairs. Cloning, the creation of self-replicating molecules in vitro, the genome projects, the potential transplant of vital organs—including memory—are and will be of such consequence as to generate mutations in the human condition. What facet of ethics, law, demography, or social policy will be immune to these reorganizations of bodily life and consciousness? Every question as to personal responsibility, identity, the life span, the right to program heredity, the limits of state intervention in the determination of gender (for military ends), and the arrest of genetic malformations is being reformulated. In the most sober perspective, the horizons of being are made to seem unbounded yet also full of menace. Any adult, responsible awareness will need access, albeit at an introductory level, pretechnically as it were, to the concepts of the new alchemy. Otherwise women and men will be excluded from indispensible political, social and personal debates. Already, the controversies raging over therapeutic abortion, euthanasia, cloning and "eugenic" manipulations demand from the layman, so intensely implicated, a considerable sophistication. To echo the old maxim: the life sciences are far too serious to be left to the scientists. The caring layman will have to do some homework if his or her voice is to be heard. Already, fundamentalist censorship, the political appeal to raucous ignorance demonstrate the urgency of the problem and the imperative need for some measure of biological-genetic literacy.

A central curriculum in mathematics, music, architecture and the life sciences. Taught, wherever possible, historically. Starting in the milieu of early schooling, the computer can make these four realms contiguous and interactive with the mind and imagination of the student. These four axes open sensibility to both the most immediate challenges and the outermost reaches of thought. Strikingly, they also embody an incommensurable potential for fun, play, and aesthetic delight. *Homo ludens* is enlisted to the turbulent heart of his being. To discern wit in mathematics, humor in music (Haydn, Satie), playfulness in architecture—that gherkin over London—or the sheer loveliness of certain molecular structures, is to participate in a pedagogy for hope. No man or woman should feel themselves to be literate in this new millennium without some grasp of a nonlinear equation, without some intimation of how music speaks its world language, without some recognition of the issues at stake, aesthetic and practical, formal and political when a new building mushrooms on the horizon and without some feel for the biogenetic reshaping of our identity (Aristotle's or Descartes's *ego* are no longer ours). How else can we be at home, or even an informed guest in what Martin Heidegger has called "the house of being"?

Any systematic, comparative study of these findings and

proposals, with their statistical evidence, would require a collaborative effort, teamwork. To this indispensable strategy I am, unfortunately, inapt. No committee has benefitted from my anarchic improprieties. Hence the time to try and do my own work.

Literacy as numerate, musical, architectural, and biogenetic. A mad project. I only wish it were more so.

| OF MAN AND BEAST |

PRESUMABLY, THE PROCESS required hundreds of thousands of years. We do not know where or how it took place. As in a gradual morning light, prehistoric hominids must have come to regard, to identify themselves as other than animal. Or, in a revolution of consciousness far greater than any since, as being animals of a special breed. Incitements to this recognition—sensory, cerebral, perhaps social, though in a tentative, fluid manner—must have arisen both pragmatically and from within the maturing recesses of the psyche. If we knew how to probe deeply enough into the nocturnal magma of what we call "the self," we might detect traces of that "big bang." Some background noise may persist at the seminal but unrecapturable edges where human rationality breaks down or in the hidden prologue to dreams. The cosmological simile is, however, misleading. There was no sudden burst, no fantastically rapid expansion. The unfolding must have come to pass in minute stages marked by innumerable regressions, by a gravitational pull backward, perhaps by a compulsive reversion to the lost comforts of animality. A million years or more may have been needed, a million years of subconscious hesitation and nostalgia prior to crossing the threshold—this is itself a simplistic image—into the singular condition at once sovereign and catastrophic of perceiving oneself as human, as an animal other than animal. One need not be a Hegelian logician to take in the shock of negativity in the assertion: "I am human, I am not non-human." This self-defining proposition is always hypothetical, always subject to psychological or moral or genetic qualification. It entails a claim to "otherness" of the most radical kind, "radical" signifying, as Marx emphasized, that which pertains to our roots.

Some of the seminal encounters with the natural order, with the fauna which teemed on the earth, often with physical strengths far greater than those of "embryonic" man, and which triggered the advance into apartness can be conjectured. Erect, endowed with stereoscopic vision, with that prehensile thumb, producing implements of increasing efficacy, the bipeds which we are began killing more often than we were killed, devouring more routinely than we were devoured. Certain anthropologists attach the determinant transition, or ought it to be "transgression," to mastery over fire. Capable of lighting and sustaining fire at will, protohistoric men and women enter a realm of planning, of foresight denied to even the most prudential of animals. Promethean creatures could now cook their food, keep warm through the winter, and have light after sundown. Other paradigms, Marxist models among them, associate the coming of man into "man" with the collective cultivation and storage of foodstuffs. These survival skills do seem to necessitate, at however transitory and rudimentary a level, an evolving degree of social organization. (Yet precisely in this respect ants and bees do rather better than *Homo sapiens*.) In essence, solitary man is not yet quite human, so Rousseau. Antique wisdom held him to be either a god or a beast.

Almost universally—there are intriguing exceptions—creation myths and philosophical anthropology draw the line between man and animal in regard to language. Man is the "language-animal" (*zoon phonanta*). Birds, whales, primates, insects have developed means of communication, some of which seems to be highly sophisticated (the semiotic dance of bees, the signal-songs of whales). But only man speaks in innovative, comprehensive ways. The origins of this decisive uniqueness exercise theological, epistemological, poetic, sociological speculations since remote antiquity. Today, the substance of argument and conjecture has shifted to comparative anatomy (the evolution of the larynx), information theory, neurophysiology, and the mapping of the human cortex. Computational simulacra, models based on the electrochemistry of synapses in the brain, generative transformational grammars have produced highly ingenious suppositions. Is it unfair to suggest that little fundamental insight has been gained? Too often these positivist algorithms assume what needs to be shown. The classical conviction that human speech is divinely bestowed and inspired is at least candid (it is majestically propounded by Hamann). The innateness postuated by generative grammars lacks all neurophysiological foundations and elides the problem of genesis. The conundrum of whether there can be conceptualization without or prior to language remains unresolved. Common ground is that of the recognition that the capacities of language to classify, to abstract from, to metaphorize reality—if indeed there is any "outside" language—constitute not only the human essence but its primordial demarcation from animality. (Again, the case of the deaf-mute embodies what may be an enigmatic crux.) We speak therefore we think, we think therefore we speak, a dynamic circularity which defines us. The "word" which was in the beginning, even stripped of its theological and mystical implications, initiated humanity. It also marked man's farewell to his animal competitors, *compagnons,* and, as it were, contemporaries. The times of women and men were to be other than those of animals. We are unable to conceive of our inward or outward condition, of knowledge or imagining, of history or society, of remembrance or futurity without language(s). This axiomatic indispensability inclines us to forget those primary functions which do not require discourse. I have pointed to the ambiguous relations between speech and sexuality. Hunger and thirst have their wordless imperatives. As does hatred. Battle cries need no syntax. But overall we are more than any animal, or more justly, we are different from any other animal, even from those primates with whom we share some ninety percent of our genome, by virtue of being able to articulate and conceptualize this finding. Animals cannot answer back. Only a mythical handful among us—Siegfried when he listens to the warning of the bird, Saint Francis when he preaches to the fish—can cross the divide into the language that is not language of animals. To himself and his fellow men, man alone speaks.

Intuition and reflection have long associated this singularity with the human apprehension of death. Men and women's linguistic endowments empower them to conceptualize and to verbalize their own mortality. Concomitantly, it has been held that animals do not possess this foreknowledge of their own passing, that they inhabit a constant present. But is this so? It is not only elephants to which both fable an direct witness attribute some prevision of their own decease, signalled by discreet withdrawal into solitude. Anyone familiar with certain domestic species, notably dogs, will have observed patterns of behavior, modulations of attitude which clearly suggest an anticipation of death. There are even among mammals phenomena which seem to reflect mourning and visitations to the remains of their departed. Again, elephants are a prime example. Correspondingly, mythologies and folklore make of animals heralds of our own decease. If death has its smell, animals detect it early. Owls hoot, ravens caw, wolves howl around the dwellings of the doomed. Achilles' horses know of this impending fate. Cats, long cherished, retreat from the scent of fatal infirmity and bristle at death. The difference seems to me to lie elsewhere. I have tried to show in *After Babel* that the vitality, the forward motion of human consciousness and social history relate intimately to the grammar of subjunctives, optatives and counterfactuals. Our semantic capacity to transcend, to negate the brute imperatives of our organic condition, to debate with death, depends on the inductive "absurdity," on the wizardry of the future tenses of the verb. By virtue of grammatical liberties, whose unfounded pretensions we rarely pause to consider, women and men can describe, can con-

verse about the day after their own deaths. They can program social aims, analyze scientific configurations millennia in the offing.
It is this syntax of futurity which looks to be quintessentially
human. Which sets us ontologically apart. Animals obviously anticipate imminent danger. They may sense earthquakes hours before these wrench our cities. My dogs shiver at thunder well before
it becomes audible to a human ear. Animals take flight, display
camouflage, dig burrows, store food. But there is nothing to suggest that they imagine "beyond themselves," that they can mentally
or symbolically accede to tomorrow. Their grammars are those of
past and present, which may be a characterization of instinct.

Nonetheless, during most of history and today still the demarcations, the borderlands remain uncertain. The understanding
that animals preceded man, that they are our ancestry is now
firmly established except among fundamentalists. Creation myths,
etiologies of human evolution invoke animal parentage. Prehistoric man was a Darwinian. In fable we are born of avian eggs, of
animal excrements, of dragons' teeth. We were suckled by wolves,
fed by commiserating ravens, carried to safety on the bounding
backs of dolphins. There could be no origins of religion, of myths
if distinctions between the human and the animal order were not
blurred and susceptible to metamorphoses. The turn to worship
began with animal representations. Anubis and the Egyptian pantheon bear the heads of animals. Early mankind seeks cosmic ordinance and tribal identity via animal totems. The totemic bear or
eagle or serpent gives immediate access, both literal and symbolic,
to the custodian powers of the supernatural. The shaman wears
the mask of the jaguar; he *is* the jaguar whom the clan meets in the
clarity of trance, of initiation to manhood. Heraldry which reaches
to the onset of modernity is a zoology. Unicorns support royal arms
and wait in wardrobes. Moreover, the world of primordial fables,
of the graphic *figurae* which marked our ripening, teems with hybrid creatures part god, part animal, part man. At no point does

imagination or the subconscious renounce its kinship with categories of being other than the strictly human. Partial as it is—the history of *Homo sapiens* is brief—the process of humanizations seems to have left deep scars and nostalgias. We have been exiled into our humanity.

Hence the vast catalog of hybrid forms. Centaurs, sirens, harpies, mermaids gallop, sing, dive-bomb, or swim their way through legends and nightmares. Birds with the faces of women, women with the tails of fish, stallions half-men tell of a world in which creation was full of rough drafts, of indiscriminacies and provisional alchemy. There are creatures who cross and recross the unmarked frontier, who transgress in the proper sense of the term. Wolf-men abound in folk and fairy tales. The separation of man from bear is tentative and susceptible to revision. Leopard-men haunt the African night. Out of Circe's swine, human eyes blink. In eschatological icons, in revelation and in the *Paradiso,* divine disclosure, the informing shapes which populate transcendent radiance assume animal likeness. There is "Christ the tiger" and the crowned eagle of pontifical and militant sovereignty. In these spheres of combinatorial possibility the divine can cohabit with both the human and the animal. It is not only that deities, whether palaeo-Siberian, Olympian or Amerindian enter into human and animal guise when they loiter among us; it is that cosmogony teems with heroic or demonic "mulattos," half-breeds, octoroons in which every conceivable amalgam of godhead and mortality, of the divine and the bestial is compounded. Provenance is a thicket. In a single outwardly human woman or man, in the children of Leda or Semele, a divine sperm, an engendering in animal form and a human recipient are inextricably meshed. In Hercules or Achilles the divine and the human lineage, the fragile fabric of humanity within the mystery of the undying create a tension at once charismatic and divisive. Those riddling "sons of God" who visit earthly women in Genesis 6, the angelic orders which have so long vexed Christian theological disputations, the "supermen" of Nietzsche's futurology and of our science fiction and comic books testify to endless blending. We are alloys. If human beings are prone to waking up as demigods, Titans, or lion-kings, they are equally in danger of waking up as cockroaches. It is no accident that Kafka's parable, more perhaps than any other, has come to be emblematic of our unsettled condition.

Consequently, the contours of sexuality remain malleable. Ethnographers, sociologists, criminologists conjecture as to what the law designates by the tawdry and crass term of "bestiality." Undoubtedly, modes of erotic intimacy and intercourse between man and beast have been perennial and widespread. Erotic familiarity between man and animal abound in the isolation of the shepherd's existence, in the hypnotic solitudes of alpine pastures or prairies. That "shudder in the loins," that momentary warmth and flush of vitality are not only the stuff of myth, of Pasiphaë and her bull, but are commonplace in the domains of agriculture, of husbandry (an interesting word), and migration. Chastened by allegory, they provide the pulse of narrative in Ovid's *Metamorphoses,* in *A Midsummer Night's Dream,* and Keats's *Lamia.* Yet so far as serious literature, let alone direct observation, goes the theme of copulation between man and animal remains virtually taboo. Among moderns it is ventured upon by D. H. Lawrence and Montherlant. A Canadian novella, by a woman writer too soon deceased, renders both plausible and deeply moving a love affair between a solitary woman and an inquisitive bear. It is a rare masterpiece. A transgressive libido permeates the oneiric jungles and moon-drenched desert of Douanier Rousseau's paintings. A scarcely veiled fantasy of sexual longing underlies the memorable kitsch of *King Kong* as it does the scabrous wit of Apuleius' *Golden Ass.* What would fair tales be without the motif, operative throughout the world, of *la belle et la bête,* of a woman's body conjoined with the fur and sheathed claws of her seducer, an embrace made the more unnerving when the beloved bids her partner resume his feline shape?

Those who have sex with an animal are in congress with their own biological and psychosomatic past. They rejoin a lost reality, at once terrifying and pastoral, in which pre-hominids and hominids had not yet divorced from the immediacies of the natural order. From the extended family of the organic. The "animal-lover" in a carnal sense escapes from the intrusive despotism, from the foreclosures of language to which I have previously alluded. In the Hungarian tale, set to music by Bartók, it is the rutting grunt of the forest buck, himself transmuted out of humanity, which compels women. And many are the fables in which bride and bridegroom, returning to their nuptial chamber, confront the loathing, the febrile vengeance of the domestic pet which now feels betrayed, whose teeth or talons are bared. As a Turkmenian proverb has it: "When you enter your bridal bed, look at the eyes of your cat."

The history of man's conduct toward animals is fragmentary. Its decisive inception escapes us. The animal representations in Paleolithic caverns, the animal statuettes carved of mammoth or walrus ivory perhaps two thousand years ago are electric with life. They are the notations of a predator among his fellow predators. Their "inscape," their penetration into the aura of animality has been matched only by Dürer and Picasso. But their intent remains hidden. Were they objects of religious veneration and propitiation meant to honor and assuage those kindred beings whom hunters had killed and consumed? Were these inspired frescoes meant to serve as bait, hoping to draw the quarry into range? Or might the wonders of Lascaux be "nothing but art" products of an instinct for mimetic creation and beauty proper to man? This act would indeed dissociate man from animals. In which case the near inaccessibility of much of cave painting poses a further problem. What is certain are the intensities of awareness, of reciprocal neighbor-

hood, of interaction whether hostile or familial which bound prehistoric communities to the horses, bears, mammoths, wolves, and
cervine quadrupeds among whom they led their auroral lives.
What followed must have been slaughter and domestication on an
immense scale and across slow millennia. Whether wild or domes-
ticated, at large or in harness, animals became men's victims and
slaves. They provided the diversions of the hunt—medieval and *ancien régime* monarchs, Edwardian nabobs, hunters on the American great plains massacred game in obscene superfluity—or the
requisites of food, clothing, tools, and ornaments. To this day, the
seas run blood-red during tuna fishing, songbirds are shotgunned
out of the sky for amusement and the remnants of endangered
species are hounded to extinction by the rich and the poacher. So
as to make the gods accomplices to our own wanton bloodlust, animal sacrifice became an inherent part of religious rites. This development is cited as humanely progressive when compared to
human sacrifice. An equivocal compliment. What was the guilt of
the ram "caught in a thicket by his horns" when Abraham "offered
him up for a burnt offering in the stead of his son"? What was the
crime of the "beauteous" heifer whose throat Odysseus cut so as to
make of its blood a lure for the thirsty spirits of the dead?

Totemic animals preside over clans; deities are worshipped in
animal guise; folk wisdom and mythologies ascribe to animals preternatural powers of anticipation, vengeance or safeguard; in the
Zodiac stars delineate animal names and contours; in moments of
lucidity we know ourselves to be no better than naked apes. Yet
who challenged Jahweh's commandment that man was to exercise
"dominion over the fish of the sea, and over the fowl of the air, and
over the cattle . . . and over every creeping thing that creepeth
upon the earth"? Moreover, it is where Buddhism, Jainism, and an-
imist faiths preach reverence for all life that the actual treatment
of animals can be most barbaric. Chinese cruelty toward and exploitation of animals remains unspeakable. Aristotle regarded it as

implausible that animals could possess any faculty corresponding to a soul. In doctrines of metempsychosis, such as Pythagoras', the fallen psyche wrestles to free itself from its punitive, transitory animal sheath so as to regain its sanctified human status. Across the earth and for thousands of years, animals have been butchered, hunted, and worked to death. Signs of human guilt were almost indiscernable. The scarcely examined priority of human eminence and well-being is taken by many to justify vivisection (a practice I find abhorrent). The notion of animal rights, of ethical responsibility toward animals, remained fitful and eccentric. The mule was left to starve or die of thirst after a lifetime's servitude; the tethered dog was abandoned to maddening fear and hunger when its owners (who *owns* an animal?) moved house. The history of the dawning of effective compassion and answerability remains obscure though a handful of social historians and philosophical anthropologists are now beginning to tease it out. Though documented instances are not frequent, protests against the torture and slaughter of animals in the arena do surface among Roman moralists and Church Fathers. Via processes only partially elucidated, animal sacrifice recedes from Judaism. (But can the Temple be restored without it?) Its rejection is one of the glories of nascent and maturing Christianity precisely where it prevailed over the blood rituals of Mithraic cults. An intermittent, largely subterranean current of sensibility precedes Franciscan tenderness toward animal life. The iconography of the lamb and the donkey as these figure in Christian symbolism and Christological parables may have played a heuristic role. The murderous hunter, such as St. Hubert, pauses and repents as he perceives a holy cross springing from between the antlers of the stricken deer. Honor is shown to the hound who, whether in legend or chronicle, has kept watch even to the point of starvation over its master's body. Reverting, perhaps subconsciously to archaic rites, great artists such as Wagner ask to be entombed next to their pets. When a dead dog is thrown into the Old Cemetery in Prague so as to defile it, the Rabbi orders its reverent burial. Such empathy and intimations of fundamental kinship are, however, sporadic and anecdotal. The Enlightenment, even in its radical vein, generates no particular sense of protection for animals. The *philosophes* tended to regard any special affection for animals as infantile sentimentality. The servitude of beast to man is axiomatic.

What has brought on current changes of perspective, significant albeit partial? Here again, the story is complicated and as yet unclear. What has inspired mutations of human feeling that now call for the protection of man-eating sharks and respect for the pit viper? Which have actually inscribed in certain legal systems prohibitions of cruelty to animals? Darwinism is of monumental importance. It is an ancient, atavistic terror at our descent from and consanguinity with animals, with primates, which fueled opposition to the theory of evolution and which continues to incense Christian fundamentalists in the United States. Molecular biology, genetics have buttressed Darwinism by demonstrating, as I have mentioned, the virtual genetic identity between humans and primates. When we do to death or maltreat animals—also the newt is among our forefathers—we commit an act of genetic patricide. Of comparable importance have been the scientific, ethological studies of animal behavior. Jane Goodall among her chimpanzees, Diana Fossey striving to save mountain gorillas from extinction, Biruté Gladikas (known as "mother of monkeys") have alerted our awareness to the social intricacies, to the wealth and pathos of the emotional lives of our more-than-cousins. We have been taught to wonder at the dance of the bees and at the imprinting which occurs when a duckling seeks out parentage. The likelihood that whales and porpoises are endowed with communicative means, with signal codes as yet beyond our adequate understanding, growing insights into the global navigational systems either celestial or magnetic whereby migrant birds span oceanic immensities have helped alter the status of animals in the hierarchies of organic being. When we look into the eyes of a chimpanzee, we are looking at a sad mirror. At an accusing mirror.

Whatever the instigations, new attitudes toward animal life, together with new valuations of the rights of children (these two may well be psychologically connected) are among the very few moral gains in modernity. A nightmare is upon us: that of a planet polluted, ravaged, exploited to the point of lunar inertness. Of catastrophes of climate unleashed by our insensate greed. Already much of the Earth has been stripped of its natural fauna. Already hundreds, probably thousands of animal species have been annihilated. Rivers, ponds, overfished seas no longer sustain the spellbinding chain of marine and aquatic life. Hunger maddens and decimates species such as the tiger, the snow leopard or the polar bear. With obscene irony, Japanese whalers massacre their prey in order to feed house pets and poachers harry rhinoceros to extinction so that their horns may furnish aphrodisiacs for moronic Chinese. Alpaca were all but eliminated to provide sweaters and scarves for Western boutiques. But more and more voices are raised in protest. These range from the criminal hysteria of certain animal-rights groups to reasoned criticism and a widely diffused sentiment of malaise, of shared guilt. We are beginning to feel lonely on this crowded Earth. The protection of wildlife, the salvation of certain species such as the oryx or the giant panda from the brink of disappearance, legislation to curb cruelty to animals do enlist a growing spectrum of individual and communal energies. The mountain lion, the black bear are afforded what protection is possible from the hunter, from the collector of "trophies." Furs are still worn in overheated Western cities, but under rising protest. Perhaps the Far East can be taught that there is better to do with dogs than eat them. The issue of the use of animals in medical research is exceedingly complicated. It raises ethical and psychological concerns of extreme delicacy. But the debate and the anger are invaluable. They tell of a seismic shift in sensibility, in man's perception of and unease over his place in creation. Whether the scream, the suffocation of an animal in a laboratory is justified by medical progress is, at the least, a question worth asking.

Devoid of any conscious or, in exceptional cases, of any subconscious sexual component, one's love for an animal can equal, can surpass any other. Have we tried to understand this? Unlike even the most passionate, devoted love between humans, love of an animal can be totally disinterested. We want to believe that animals are capable of developing some modes of affection toward us, that they can "love" in return. They do manifest signs of reciprocal need, of affectionate dependence, of fidelity (Odysseus' dog). But these reflexes may, to a significant degree, be desiderata on our part, metaphoric and anthropomorphic conceits. Can we ever be certain? What can be absolute is our love for the animal or animals in our lives, asking for no guaranteed return. It is part of the strange logic of this absolute that almost any animal can become its object. Elephants, horses, goats, but also hamsters, parrots, and canaries have elicited human love and heartbreak. The death of a goldfish, of a finch, may leave children, but also the elderly, traumatized and suddenly cognizant of the concordances between love and death. Men have risked their lives in order to rescue from a burning house their cherished python. To plunge into freezing or stormy waters to retrieve one's dog is commonplace. It is, for so many of us, dogs who embody the folly of utter human devotion. Cats are another kingdom. Whether at the feet of Richelieu, whether in the guise of Colette's Mitsou or that of dazzling Snowball on my French translator's desk, they answer our affection with irony, with observant detachment. Something in their ancient eyes finds our love a touch ridiculous. Dogs can be loved with every nerve and fiber of one's being. Their mien can become a talisman of mutual recognition. They seem to reflect in mysterious foresight both their own incipient death and ours. We listen for, we identify the step of our dog, his or her bark, the growl emitted in half-sleep as we do our own heartbeat. When our dog dies, our existence fractures. The house turns empty. The blanket, the bowl left behind seem unbearable. Fascinatingly, this condition seems to have eluded Shakespeare's otherwise encompassing register of human reflexes.

A troubling paradox attaches to this love. There are those, possibly numerous, who cherish animals more than they do human beings. This truth is rarely discussed. The illness or death of an animal may solicit depths of emotion beyond those occasioned by human infirmity. The pain of animals, even at a distance, blackens my mind. In her fine book on tigers, Ruth Padel, poet and voyager, reports the screams of a boa constrictor being skinned alive. I wish to God that I had never read that passage. It sickens my dreams, also in daylight. To cherish animals more than men may testify to some visceral though undeclared contempt for man's inhumanity, for his "bestiality." There is an intuition that animals may possess a dignity, a loyalty, an endurance under pain and injustice denied to all but a handful of women and men. This might account for the disturbing fact that a particularly acute love and compassion for animals occurs in men of a despotic and hateful ideological temper. They are not a reassuring lot: Caligula and his horse; Wagner and his Newfoundland; Nietzsche's mental collapse at the sight of a horse being flogged; Hitler, if legend is correct, wept when his beloved Alsatian, Blondie, had to be put down in the hell of the bunker. I have every reason to believe that I am a physical coward, a bourgeois mandarin repelled and frightened by violence. Yet I *know* that if danger threatened my dog, if anyone offered him hurt, my rage, my impulse to interpose could turn homicidal. If torturers set about my wife or children, I would cry out to them to hold fast and strive to do so myself. Were they to beat my dog or put out his eyes, I would break immediately, betraying all. These are not comely truths. They defy reason and what should be the hierarchies of human love. They raise questions as to primordial instabilities, as to the survival of the zoological affinities and twilight which subvert our fragile humanity. They are truths nevertheless. Shared, I suspect, by many more of us than is openly admitted. Odysseus bids adieu to Penelope not long after his epic homecoming. Would he have left Ithaka had his dog Argos lived?

A warm blizzard engulfed us. My two young children had seen pictures of an Old English sheepdog, also known as Bobtails, in a Sunday color supplement. Rightly, my wife had pointed out that this would be too large a breed for our house, that its opulent fur would require perpetual brushing, that there was about this entire creature a touch of absurdity, an air of a James Thurber cartoon. We must look to something reasonable. What was wrong with Golden Retrievers? Pure chance had it that breeders of Old English sheepdogs had their home only a few streets away. What harm in having a look? There we sat when the door to the parlour flung open. Five joyous monsters tumbled over us. Son and daughter vanished, squealing with delight in a turbulence of gray and white and blueish fur, of pitch-black noses and improbable paws. The patriarch, one Markus, camped on my wife's lap. Eyes like black pearls, a whirlwind of imperious affection canceling out any Darwinian precepts about the survival of the fittest or adaptive niches. Then the glorious pack, three generations deep, settled at our feet and looked up at us. How could we even consider any other kind? My wife had tears of laughter and acceptance on her cheeks.

Came the puppy. So small, so wobbly on its furry paws that it could barely master the distance between our children as they knelt in the garden. A few weeks later, coming home, we found the garden door accidentally off is latch. Had the puppy gone astray? Never will I forget the sheer anguish in my wife's voice, the ache as she called out its name. After a few interminable moments, the white tufts came racing out of the dark.

Rowena, the Lady Rowena (Sir Walter Scott loomed large in our David and Deborah's reading) grew to regal splendor. The shades of gray, of white, the nuances of gray blue shone even in moonlight. She trained us thoroughly. An Old English sheepdog is present, can be gently or haughtily exacting, twenty-five hours a day. Words cannot render the ways in which even its sleep gives to the house a warm hum, a pervasive pitch of presence. Rowena taught us that the clump hanging from her paw was not an open wound—we had of course rushed to the vet in high alarm—but simply frozen mud. At the time I was teaching abroad and commuting. She would sadden and bristle at the sight of my luggage and turn to the front door in excitement at the hour in which I left the Geneva airport to return home (human beings emit smells of expectation). Parting has its scent. Dame Rowena's ancestry was that of working dogs herding cattle on the Welsh uplands. But the mournful cows we encountered in our walks along the river Cam filled her with a certain apprehension. The shadings of her attitudes when meeting other dogs were as varied and hierarchic as any in the *Almanach de Gotha*. She acknowledged as her peer a sovereign Irish Setter, she exhibited a slightly condescending regard for the obviously sagacious Labrador down the road. Small yappers, occasional lurchers, spaniels provoked her more or less benign scorn. Dogs suffer from nightmares: Rowena would quiver in her sleep, wake bewildered and crouch by me for comfort. The slightest affliction could trigger manifest gloom. Nothing on God's earth is sorrier for itself than a bobtail in discomfort or when feeling misunderstood. Once, and once only, we booked her into a kennel. Rowena stretched out on the driveway leading to its gates and would not budge. My wife and I stared at each other in guilt, the children burst into tears and the planned holiday was over. I shall never forget the mien of judgmental forgiveness with which the dog climbed back into the car. Customarily this demanding breed does not age beyond ten or twelve years. My wife, who had never owned a quadruped of any species, turned into an acutely perceptive, expert handler (she is also a great historian but that seems more routine!). Rowena lived to be sixteen. When, during an afternoon sortie, she signaled to us that her strength was ebbing, we had to take her to be put down. My nerve failed utterly. Zara was there to see her enter sleep. After which we sat in our car helpless with grief. A world had collapsed.

We picked Jemima from a litter in Gloucestershire. Even as a puppy her elegance, the nervous vivacity of her motions were unmistakable. But she had been too closely bred. All manner of noises, of unprepared meetings frightened her. She was capricious, almost feline in her moods and affections. Prickly about her diet. Succesive attempts at mating Jemima proved an almost comical fiasco. She seemed to regard the entire process as beneath her mercurial dignity. When she tossed her head, she had the air of one of those vibrant heraldic hounds drawn by Pisanello. We cherished her but never overcame the impression that Jemima was a guest, a transient out of a domain of fabled creatures only partly accessible to us. She did not attain a great age.

If the word "sweetness" has meaning, it pertains to Lucy. She was a rescue dog, small in size but with a boundless heart. She may have known hurt before she came to us. Her markings were delicate, with soft tufts of beige. Her contentment in having found a good home was manifest. I have never known an animal more gently disposed, more anxious to adapt. She delighted in children, they in her. Loud noises made her flinch (Jemima had taken fierce umbrage at the clanking of garbage trucks and cans). There was not an aggressive bone in Lucy's compact frame, not a hostile impulse in her luminous being. She passed away in serene sleep, her paw curled in a characteristic posture of welcome.

As I write, Ben rules. He presides over our daily lives. The first male after our three bitches he is leonine in his strength and lunge. Impossible to restrain on a leash when in pursuit of cats, squirrels or clamorous crows. Ben is a mafioso demanding respect, capable of baring his scimitar teeth. Yet by far the most demonstrably affectionate of the lot. Prone to climb on one's lap, to proffer his shaggy paw in salutation and caress. Totally at ease with whomever he encounters or comes to the door. An adroit exploiter of our every indulgence, bartering the shoes, the slippers he absconds with for a biscuit, sulking when there is not television backdrop to his evening drowse. Ben's internal chronometer is flawless: he acts on his chosen habitual hours with total exactitude, whether it is at meal time or lights out. His musical taste is discriminatory. He balks at brass bands and emits a low growl when Ravel's *Bolero* comes on. He is at peace with Haydn and all manner of baroque instrumentalists. Having figured in photographs and portraits made during interviews, having graced the cover of a prestigious literary journal, Ben has a certain renown. He has been described as "the charismatic *Monsieur Ben*" (Lucy would have hidden). He seems fully aware of his status. It may incite his magisterial behavior towards other dogs. Lap dogs, miniature terriers, yappers excite his somewhat menacing contempt. There have been incidents (the young police officer who came to inquire melted into Ben's perceptive embrace). It is not, however, the dogs who focus his interest. It is their masters whom he seeks out in great bounds. Ben banks on his irresistibility and is rarely frustrated. Fireworks and thunder are his bane, but despite their thumping march the Christmas visit by the Salvation Army provokes reciprocal joy. Ben is inexcusably exigent. When we leave him in the house even briefly, his look of stricken reproach would turn Medusa to stone. He reads our every mood, echoing, miming after his own fashion our sorrows or happiness. He fills our days. I know that Ben too will leave us before too long. Just now I cannot conceive of being without him.

I have wanted to write, to illustrate a book about these four intimates. It is not difficult to make of animals megaphones for human voices as do Aesop or La Fontaine. To invent a Babar or a Bambi. It is immensely difficult to render plausible what we intuit of an animal's inward identity, of the view it takes of us. I had hoped to write a fairy-tale sequence for my two granddaughters. There would be a dream-shop where Rowena, Jemmy, Lucy, and Ben gather during the long nights, consuming an Aladdin's cave of chocolate drops without ever being sick. Or a wizard's garden in which *they* are the masters. I had hoped to persuade my Rebecca and my Miriam, also myself, that there is an Arcadia after death in which we shall be reunited. Those who have succeeded in writing such tales, who have heard the wind whistle in the willows and the wolves whisper are altogether exceptional. They are writers of genius (Jack London, Rudyard Kipling, Virginia Woolf, Colette). The child has endured in them—and an enviable strangeness. I am hardly of their number.

But it is my conviction that human cruelty, lust, territorial rapacity, and arrogance exceed those of the animal order. Our maltreatment of animals, the insensate hecatombs to which we resort, as during the foot-and-mouth panic, are symptomatic of tyrannical blindness or indifference. There is, as I have said, no corner of the Earth in which, every day and at every hour, animals are not beaten, worked to wretched death, or hunted for entertainment (the word "game" is eloquent). It is as if man was possessed by the will to wipe out what vestiges remain of a lost Eden. These seem to remind him unbearably of some original lapse from innocence, from universal companionship. So long as we humiliate and massacre animals, so long as we refuse to read the signals of premonition and suffering in their eyes, there will be no end to our politics of hatred and internecine ruin. Perhaps there is still time. Natural disasters appear to be multiplying: tidal waves, volcanic eruptions, earthquakes, lethal rock-falls, and mud slides. It is as if an abused, trashed Earth were in rebellion. That the organic world, of which animals are so essential a component, may be tiring of man's wasteful, predatory dominion. Where polluting mills have closed down in northern New England, the forests have returned. Kites nest on the cornices of our high-rise buildings. Once hunted to near-extinction, wild boar grunt in European woods. Salmon have been seen in the Hudson.

I am aware of what may be confused and irrational in these persuasions. I do eat meat. I benefit from medical progress associated with experiments on animals. There is undoubtedly in the love I have felt for my dogs over these past thirty years a strain of sentimentality, of self-indulgent pathos. My grief over the loss of these good companions is somehow sharper, more prolonged than that which I feel in regard to all but a handful of intimates. This may point to an emotional defect, to immaturity in my own psyche. It may relate to a child's desolation over the loss of his stuffed teddy bear. If I have anything to bequeath after my death (doubtful), it should but very probably won't go to the destitute or the protection of children, but to the schooling of seeing-eye dogs for the blind. They are glorious creatures. They need retirement homes. I take no pride in these choices. They are, indefensibly perhaps, non-negotiable. Are they what is least Jewish in me?

To write my "animal book" would have required not only eminent psychological and narrative skills. It would have necessitated raw introspection. I did not have the guts.

| BEGGING THE QUESTION |

THOSE GENEROUS ENOUGH to be interested in my work or adverse to it have often posed the same question. After reading my books, during seminars, or following public lectures, either with hesitant politeness or with reproach: "What are your politics? In all your writings on history and culture, on education and barbarism, why is there no frank statement of your own political ideology? Where do you really take your stand?" I know that this challenge and the malaise which it implies are legitimate. What is more damaging: I remain uncertain as to the psychological roots of my reticence or evasion. The external facts are clear enough. At no time in my life have I been politically active, have I joined this party or that. No political program, no partisan movement has engaged my support, insignificant as it might be. I have not voted in any election, local or national. If there is a single exception to these abstentions it is my declared anguish over Zionism and certain of Israel's policies set out in a preceding chapter. Otherwise my conduct, my writings, my teaching have been those of one whom Aristotle would characterize as an "idiot," the man who stays home, who refuses to become involved in the affairs and responsibilities of the city. Though he realizes that this refusal, this adherence to privacy empowers and, in a sense justifies, the access to government, to public office of the despotic, of the corrupt and the mediocre. Choosing to be "housebound," the man or of late the woman who refuses any participation in the political process is, in essence, a voyeur. He or she makes of the forces—which in fact shape much of one's existence—a spectator sport. Strictly considered, only the hermit has earned the right to such detachment. Only solitude can be extraterritorial to the body politic. But even then there are ambiguities and contamintions (set out classically in Thoreau's *Walden*). The polis is never far away. Montaigne will become mayor of Bordeaux.

What myopia, what autistic impulse has led me to regard every collective, be it a committee or a mob, a learned academy or a team, as inherently suspect? What cautionary arrogance or acedia has made me "unclubbable" and persuaded me that I must be mouthing platitudes or inanities if others agree with me? Why have I refused to add my signature to manifestos, appeals, protests with many of whose propositions and urgencies I concur? The high masters of aloneness, a Kierkegaard or a Nietzsche or a Wittgenstein, have their reasons. But what of someone like myself, someone acutely aware of the paradox that the political machinery in which he refuses to take part very often guarantees the license, the immunities of this refusal? Both democracy and tyranny, each in their own lights, allow passivity.

I can guess at circumstantial, autobiographical motives. Coming of age under the lunatic menace of fascism and of Nazism, convinced by my father's pellucid insight that utopian socialism and Marxism-Leninism would end, and end rapidly, in enslavement, I was from the outset wary of the political. This wariness was reinforced by that condition of peregrine Judaism, by the feeling of being a tentative, even unwelcome guest, which I have outlined earlier. Should a guest intervene in family quarrels? Add to this the ironies of my father in respect of electoral processes. Time and again he would cite Goethe's maxim that a "political tune is a vile tune" (*ein garstig Lied*). Yet these very factors should have oriented me toward passionate support for the "open society," for democratic, liberal institutions such as I found and benefited from when taking refuge in the United States and completing my education in England. It is precisely my awareness of totalitarian eventualities and Jewish marginality in the diaspora which should have enlisted me in ardent defense of tolerant democracy or, indeed, of some mode of democratic socialism on, say, the Scandinavian model. Instead, I kept almost totally apart. Dante's haughty phrase is "to be a party of one." Why?

What I sense as being crucial is an obsession with privacy. By definition, the political cause and commitment are public, *res publica*. In essence the political is the negation of the private, although it may well be its enabling framework. An almost pathological revulsion at the curtailments of privacy in modern life—be they the calculated indiscretions of psychoanalysis, the invasive probings of bureaucracy, the exposure of bodily intimacies on the mass media, the confessional in literature, in social intercourse—has long possessed me. When I chance on them, "reality shows," now dominating television, sicken me. Questionaires, officious documents to be filled out, the rampant vulgarities of interviewers and inquisitors, the "candid camera," and the yapping of the phone seem to me to be the nightmare unleashed by the technologies of information. Bear in mind the meanings of the term "informer." In the name of clinical efficacy, of national security, of fiscal transparency our private lives are scrutinized, recorded and manipulated. Concomitantly, the arts of solitude, of guarded discretion, of that inviolate silence which Pascal placed at the heart of true civility and adulthood have withered. It has been estimated that an average walker in the streets of central London is photographed some three hundred times by hidden surveillance cameras. To manifest my political persuasions—assuming that they might be of interest to anyone—has seemed to me to be a fundamental breach of privacy. Political spectacles and rhetoric, whether democratic or totalitarian, are kindred to a nudist colony. Yet how can there be a private politics (the question relates disturbingly to Wittgenstein's critique of "private language")?

What meaning attaches to the proposition that all women and men are created equal, which is the axiomatic anchorage of democracy?

Today, artificial insemination, cloning and other rapidly developing genetic techniques infringe upon even this problematic biological platitude. Theologically, this belief can be justified. Created in
God's image, whatever that may mean, all mortals stand equal before Him. They are always, whatever their mundane status, of infinite and equal ontological worth. His alone is any terminal
classification. It is also rationally possible to affirm that all of us
are, or should be, equal before the law. To be sure, and from the
earliest recorded history onward, this assertion has been a utopian
fiction. The fortunate, the powerful, the moneyed have never faced
the same legal apparatus as the destitute and the servile. The law,
however draconian or enlightened, is riddled with compromises
and inequities. The literate, the adroitly counseled, and the eloquent experience and exploit legislation as the poor and the
speechless cannot. Nonetheless, the abstract desideratum and
ideal does have significance. Certain societies labor more honestly
than others to achieve it. But where else, outside theological
dogma or judiciary principles, is there equality?

We are thrust into this world profoundly unequal. To be born
in the starving backlands of Cameroon is a destiny, a "truth condition" vastly different from that of the newborn even in the less
privileged sections of Manhattan. Those born blind or deaf inhabit
provinces of life immensely different from those of a "normal" individual. To be physically handicapped is to live existentially and
in countless different ways a life other than that of those who are
unimpaired (I know). Mental infirmities, often inherited, render
the gap more drastic. Genetically transmitted disease is the
damnation of the innocent, inherited capacities or wealth or special standing are the blessings of the undeserving. Beauty, an uncanny resource, is distributed randomly. What equality obtains as
between the talents of the prodigy, be they athletic, cerebral, performative, and the stumbling of the moron? Except in a formal, virtually trivial sense, it is an absurd delusion to regard as equal my

intellectual means, my sensibility, my expressive findings with those of a Plato, a Gauss or a Schubert. Conversely it is cant to equate my own resources and instrumentalities, modest as they indubitably are, with those of the subliterate, of the brain-starved and emotionally barbarized. What equality is there—again, except in religious faith or legal fiction—between an overeducated, privileged, often leisured creature like myself and the hoodlum, the addict, the vacant fanatic drifting in the slum? How can any political creed founded on axioms of human equality be other than edenic revery or self-delusion?

On the evolutionary time scale and measured against the age of the planet, *Homo sapiens* is a very late arrival. Our history is that of the blink of an eye. The limitations, the potentialities of our mental and physical resources remain largely conjectural. It may well be, as Heidegger taught, that we have not yet begun to know how to think adequately. It may be that we are groping at the doors of incipient humaneness, that our experience hitherto has been a rough sketch. The evidence is contradictory. Our species is prone to utter sadism. It tortures, it rapes, it massacres, it humiliates. There appear to be no inbuilt limitations to our sexual appetites; men abuse and rape infants. We are capable of cannibalism and homicidal greed. We blind, castrate, and bury alive helpless prisoners, be it in Cambodia or the Balkans. Experiments have shown that carefully calibrated pressures and rewards can turn a normally charitable, sophisticated individual into a torturer. Equable individuals melt into the bloodlust of a mob, slaughtering their longtime neighbors for demented or wholly contrived reasons. Throughout so-called civilizations men beat women, enslave children, maim animals—often for the mere sport and pleasure of the thing. *La bête humaine* is, as I have argued, a defamation of animals. On the other hand, women and men are not only endowed with luminous intellectual and aesthetic creativity but with compassion, with altruism and impulses to self-sacrifice. They will give away their life jackets on sinking ships, return to burning houses in order to rescue those trapped within, share their last bite in the death camps. They are capable of fantastic heroism and loyalty, of a sense of human solidarity which will lead them to affront certain death. Abstrusely speculative issues have led men and women to the stake. History abounds in hopeless uprisings against tyranny and social injustice. Politics can produce moral eminence. There has been an Abraham Lincoln, a Gandhi, a Mandela. Above all, there are the mysteries of love, of disinterested passion, the gift of self without hope of compensation. To seek to circumscribe the spaces and diversities of love is to seek to index the ocean. We can only conjecture, by anthropomorphic similitudes, whether any other species is comparably possessed. The sum of insight seems to be that the human species is, unpredictably, better and worse, more bestial and more evolved than we know. We are, as the phrase has it, "crooked wood." But we can blaze into decency and excellence.

This is the raw material all politics has to deal with. There is no other.

Teaching, lecturing, reportage have taken me to numerous societies which were at the time, or are still, under more or less totalitarian rule. These included Battista's Cuba, the Portugal of Salazar, Franco's Spain, and apartheid South Africa. I have visited the Soviet Union and post-Mao China. Repeatedly, invitations took me to Prague, Budapest, Warsaw, and Krakow then under various degrees of pseudo-Stalinist control. I gave seminars and lectures in what was the German Democratic Republic, traversing from one world to another at Checkpoint Charlie in divided Berlin. I have glimpsed theocratic absolutism in Morocco. These experiences have suggested two main suppositions. Usually despotism is the ostentatious tip of the iceberg. The great mass of life continues underneath (I have not been to lunatic extremes such as North Korea). Except during gusts of dictatorial madness and alleged peril, the "Caligula moments," the bulk of common humanity carries on in more or less habitual fashion. Licensed spheres of scientific, artistic, intellectual production can continue and even flourish. Academic research in art history, classics, musicology and medicine persisted in the Third Reich, often at a distinguished level. An extensive volume of musical training, of theatrical performance, of research in mathematics and physics, and of athletic prowess was produced under the boot of Stalinism. Very often it is censorship which ignites original genius. "Squeeze us, for we are olives," opined Joyce. On a daily scale, women and men get on with their ordinary lives affected only intermittently by the context of despotism. This was unquestionably so during Hitler's rule and across extensive stretches of normal existence under Stalin, Mussolini, and Franco. The key is that of domesticity. Where it is possible to sustain an area of "housedness," of familial routine, the psyche endures. One abdicates from the political. My second supposition is this: for the great majority of us, priorities, determinant essentials, are those of safety in our streets, of decent health care, of sound schooling for our children, and, first and foremost, of provisions for old age, of a secure retirement. It is these we look for at the hands of state bureaucracy. Where they are forthcoming, acceptance is the rational option.

A tiny minority looks higher. It finds itself suffocating under the denial of free speech, of unchecked travel, of the right to publication and electoral change. It adheres to ideals of political justice and open debate. It knows that the Gulag represents a hideous scandal. But I repeat: these vital passions and aims are the lifeblood of the very few. They hardly touch the masses. Indeed, a fact sardonically exploited by Stalin and Mao, they inspire in the community at large feelings either of indifference or of brute resentment. The coal miner, cherished by the state apparatus, all too cheerily will smash the skulls of what he takes to be a parasitic, effete intelligentsia. This manipulated dialectic is perennially functional in anti-Semitism where it smoulders under state patronage. When insurrection comes, if it comes at all, when "the walls come tumbling down," the motives are hardly those of intellectual, artistic freedom. They are not even those of any hammering desire for participation in any parliamentary process. They are bred of rage, of disgust at the corruption and inefficacy of the ruling caste. The contract with security has been broken. Food is lacking, homes go unheated, transport totters and, above all, pensions are no longer assured. Ironically, it is after "velvet revolutions" and rapture, it is after liberation that nostalgia sets in. The old despotic order had its infernal features but it did guarantee full employment, free hospitalization, and a dignified old age. These are swept away by the liberties of the free market. Newspapers are now at liberty to publish what quality news or trash they wish, the entrepreneurial mafia blossoms, but there are no jobs, emigration looks to be the only future and old age has become a nightmare. The pendulum motion of embittered remembrance is manifest in eastern Germany, in the Ukraine. Even the terrors of Stalinism can foster regrets.

The virtues of democracy are in theory irrefutable. Even despotism pays hypocritical tribute to the term. They are those of enfranchised, constitutional, legally underwritten liberties. The exercise of power is shared and constrained by participatory approval. Democratic ideals make possible not only the deployment of personal potentialities but, in materially equipped societies, an unprecedented progress in standards of living, in scientific and technological creativity. Dynamics of social mobility, of investment in education, in medical advances constitute the "quiet drama"—I am thinking of a passage in Plato's *Laws*—of democracy. Whatever local setbacks, the escalator of opportunity hums upward from generation to generation. The condition of the common man will be more prosperous, more secure, more blessed with opportunities of choice tomorrow than it is today. "Bliss is it in that dawn to be alive," testified Wordsworth when revolution came to France. Who would deny that grave problems persist? That social actualities often fall drastically short of the democratic promise? Even in America millions remain in poverty and fall outside the safety net of minimal health insurance. Elections are all too often spectral. A third of the eligible electorate sufficed to choose an American president. Running for public office demands outrageous wealth. It is a pursuit open only to the few and, all too frequently, the corruptible. Sadistic anomalies mushroom within legalism: after more than twenty years on death row, a blind and crippled convict is ceremonially executed. Egalitarianism can, as I have argued, reduce mass education to a sham. Within parliamentary democracies, be they in western Europe or the United States, racial tensions and discriminations turn out to be almost intractable. However, within the democratic dispensation these infirmities are subject to challenge, to free critique, to potential amendment. No other political theory or practice carries within itself institutional means toward positive change. Slavery has been abolished; so, in many democratic nations, has capital punishment. Democracy pays a matchless compliment to the hopes of man. Only a fool would not know this or value it profoundly.

And yet. Certain contrarieties between democracy and excellence in the life of the mind may be intrinsic. Democracy, a commitment to the majority, blow their fanfare for the common man. Whose God is, across so much of the planet, soccer. The Enlightenment creed, the meliorism of the nineteenth century which held mass schooling to be the assured road to cultural advancement, to political wisdom have proved largely illusory. The pursuit of social justice has leveled downward. Even within the ferocities of Stalinism the prestige of learning, of a quasi-Talmudic literacy, the commitment, often traumatically brutal, to the supremacy of ideas in human affairs, endured. Today, in the mass-consumption, mass-media democracies of the West and the developing world, it is no longer possible to separate political liberalism and representative government from capitalism. There have been ardent efforts to find a "third way." A humanized, socialized capitalism has obtained sporadically in such bucolic singularities as Scandinavia and Switzerland. But in pluralistic, mature democracies the imperium is that of money. In the proper, neutral sense of the term, the power relations are those of more or less undisguised plutocracy. Money exults in its crass omnipotence. It seeps into every crevice of public and private existence. The worship of the soccer player, the idolatry of the pop star, and the ostenation of the tycoon reflect their crazy wealth. Concomitantly, contempt for and indifference toward intellectual passions and creativity where these are not remunerative are precisely concordant with financial hierarchies. The painter is taken seriously when the hype of the media ascribes to his work monetary value. On the bourse of historical greats a recent survey places Shakespeare and Newton far below David Beckham and Madonna. The hunt after wealth, the dreams and envious awe which it inspires press on private lives even at their most intimate (Balzac, Ezra Pound in the *Usura* Canto dramatize this demonic infection). Relations within the bourgeois household, the games of love and of sex are saturated with deliberate or unexamined fiscal motivations. Consider the monetarization, the distortion toward a purely material significance of the word "worth." What is the "worth" of a bankrupt? Here Marx saw deeper than Freud. The coercion which the police state exercises on thought and art is indeed appalling. Yet the damage done may, in the final analysis, be no greater than that caused by the absolutism of the mass market. The quality bookshop, the "little magazine," the estoteric or minority domain in academic teaching and research, the avant-garde music label persist, if at all, on sufferance, on private largesse (admirable in America, often grudging and disdainful elsewhere). The censorship which profit imposes on the media is as destructive, perhaps more so than that of political despotism. Populist, technocratic democracy has become the right to make money and yet more money beyond any rational need or human dignity. Hence the often violent disenchantment of the young and their mounting abstention from the civic process. Lenin did know at least that gold would be best used for toilet seats.

My politics are those of privacy and intellectual obsession. They look to Dante's immemorial summons voiced by Ulysses: "we are not formed to live like brutes, *come bruta,* but to follow virtue and knowledge wherever these may lead, at whatever personal or social cost." It may be that such a conviction is in certain regards pathological and self-indulgent. Uncompromising thought, artistic and scientific immersion are, it may be, cancers of the spirit. They make of social justice "a small justice." They are too often at home in the darkness of our condition. At the same time, they seem to me to justify man, to generate his fitful ascent out of the inhuman. All I hope for from any political regime is that it allows breathing space for such obsessions, breathing space for what may not be utilitarian or collectively beneficial. That it respects dissent, also from money. I am hoping for some safeguard for the mutinous privacies of that "party of one." That every possible door be thrown open to the gifted. At best, I think of myself as a Platonic anarchist. It is not a winning ticket.

In genteel circles any direct inquiry as to one's personal religious beliefs or lack thereof was long regarded as an uncouth intrusion. On this issue privacy was allowed its sanctum. A salutary inhibition acknowledging the truth that when it comes to religious feelings most honest speakers fumble or resort to an idiom which belongs to the prehistory of reason. Here as well conventions have altered dramatically. Discretion is becoming antiquated. Public exposure, confession are becoming the grist of gossip, precisely as in regard to sex (the correlations between these two exhibitions are at once striking and difficult to analyze). As I noted, a private politics is probably a contradiction in terms. The sphere of the religious seems to me altogether different. In either affirmation or denial, it incarnates, it ought to incarnate, the innermost, the citadel of unmasked consciousness. It should be guarded in the inviolate sanctuary of the self, even where that sanctuary is empty, where it is inhabited by that active, vibrant emptiness which was that of the holy of holies in the tabernacle. If there is anything entitled to final privacy, to enclosure in heart and mind, it is surely one's personal faith as it ripens toward the solipsism of death or the dismissal thereof. Publication, in the direct sense of the term, is an irremediable devaluation, a striptease of what we call for lack of a better name "the soul," the quick and core of our labyrinthine being. It enacts, or so I have held, a tawdry paradox: self-violation, a rape of the self. What nakedness is more vulgar (as I write these lines, competitive masturbation figures on television).

This indiscretion moreover is trivialized, is falsified by the mere process of verbal expression. By being put into words, even where such words are poetically and philosophically inspired, even where thought sings. It is at the summits of religious discourse, of metaphysical and theological argument, it is where metaphor, allegory, symbolism and analogy weave their ecstatic round, as in Dante's *Paradiso* or the Psalms—that language hammers against its own ineluctable limitations. In the hands of the great writers and thinkers, of those who could produce the book of Job, Augustine's *Confessions,* the *Commedia,* or Pascal's notes, in the hands of a Kierkegaard or a Hopkins, language does appear to overreach itself, to "break through" to the otherwise inexpressible. But this self-surpassing is illusory. It is a wondrous effect of rhetoric, of stylistic ingenuity. Language with respect to religious experience can never say more than itself. Ontological affirmations, celebrations of the transcendent are tautological. They voice what they set out to voice in circularity however radiant (again, the commanding image is Dante's, together with its *reprise* in T. S. Eliot's *Four Quartets*). Vast as are its means of suggestion and figuration, no linguistic instrument can exceed the reach of its lexical and grammatical resources. These, in turn, are historically, socially, formally generated and circumscribed. When it labors to speak of "God," language mirrors itself. Which may account for the opaque sadness which can be heard from deep within even the most exultant of prayers. Even at its metaphysical-poetic summits, definitional articulations of the divine are sublime chitchat, what Heidegger qualified as *Gerede*. To which, over prolix millennia, "sages in God's holy fire," prophets, psalmists and divines have answered: "One can speak of God indirectly, via image and analogy, via inferences of logic or ecstasy. The *mysterium* of language has been bestowed on man so that he can proclaim, argue, and systematize his religious intuitions and creed. The very confines of this endowment bear witness to God's unfathomable 'otherness.' "

Even at its subtlest, in Aquinas or Maimonides, this thesis remains no more than self-fulfilling. It is sophistry, though of a lofty, profoundly felt tenor. Metaphoric constructs, similitudes, analogies, ontological proofs—so seductively astute in St. Anselm or Descartes—are the danse of the Dervish. They quicken reason and desire into trance. They can never step outside the perimeter of their own overdeterminant motion. The questions are those which language poses to itself, which the mind formulates in inward dialogue. The answers are already programmed within language itself, perhaps as it were within the map of the cortex. We know the answer as we ask the question, as we "beg the question," a revealing idiom. As that rabbinical dialectician Karl Marx observed: mankind poses only those questions to which it already has, or will have, an answer. We have nothing new to say of "God," though there may be novel ingenuities in the saying. Our theologies, our liturgies are combinatorial variants on wholly perennial themes. Hence the feverish quest for primary revelations, for initial authority, for a message or even a single letter graven in stone. Yet any such revelation, any such quest for the mystique of the infallible is nothing more than a speech-act on the human scale and within the constraints of human contingency. It is just those "tellers of the tale" who are most dubious of language, who are most economical with its fallible, shopworn usages—a Kafka, a Beckett—who seem most honest, whose abstentions from certitude cut deepest.

What of nonverbal attempts to represent, to conceptualize, to substantiate the divine? What of communicative, performative media outside the prepackaged feedback of language? From remotest prehistory onward, the human species has imaged its deities. The megalithic figurine, the fertility goddesses of the Cyclades and the Sistine Chapel frescoes of a bearded Creator in full flight are existentially equivalent. Without religious art everywhere on the planet our sensibility would be beggared, our inner and external landscapes immeasurably impoverished. Praxiteles' marble gods, the mosaics of Byzantium, the totemic masks and figurations out of Africa and the South Seas, Tantric abstraction and the smile of the Buddha are products of the sinews of the human hand and imagination, of its provisions of awe at full stretch. They spring from *human* consciousness and mimicry. "If cattle had gods, they would depict them with horns," observed the pre-Socratics. The gods are wrought in man's image. An inevitable modulation and confusion ensue. The graphics, the statuary, the lineaments of the sacred assume real presence. The representation becomes its own object. The worshiper presses his lips to the bronze toe, he embraces the sanctified icon, he bows not before the symbol but before what he takes to be its incarnation. What imminence of God can be more palpable than that which emanates from the pictorial

intensity of the Grünwald triptych? It is in denial of this assimilation of image to substance and of consequent idolatry that certain
faiths forbid graphic representations of their god. In Mosaic Judaism, in branches of Islam, in classical Puritanism, iconoclasm
prevails. Let the statue or the painting not lead us into temptation.
May He remain unimaginable in the full sense of that epithet. If
there has to be representation and formal analogy, let it be that of
abstract, nonfigurative lineaments. In Islamic calligraphy one
senses a choreography of reverence, of a meditation on the divine
which is in motion. The most concentrated, adult intimations of
supernatural proximity I have experienced are those within the
silent emptiness, in the animate spaces of the blue Mosque in Istanbul and in the broken apse of a Carolingian shrine, abandoned,
lost to all notice in a valley in Burgundy. Comparison with certain
mystical texts may be apposite. It is the sparest, those most alert to
their own failure which come closest (as in Meister Eckehart or
certain koans). Even at its most reticent and abstract, even where
it strives for severe abstention from confusions between symbol
and embodiment, however, art can tell us nothing of the actual existence or nature of a deity. It can prove nothing either way. It is
precisely where the icon, the totem, the figurine are held to be sacred, that religious feeling drifts into unexamined ritual. In that
perspective, outrageously perhaps, the frescoes of Giotto or the
Christology of Raphael are "primitive." They engender resplen-
dent illusions.

There is music. Of all expressive and executive means other
than the notations of pure mathematics, music alone cuts through
the barbed wire of language. As I have suggested, music is
supremely meaningful but its meanings remain undefinable and
refuse either paraphrase or translation. Like the tautological "I
am" out of the Burning Bush, it is what it is. Its signifying existence
is universal. Many have sought to define its indispensability, its
overwhelming potency. Schopenhauer proposes that music will

endure beyond the extinction of our world; for Lévi-Strauss melody is "the supreme mystery." For innumerable men and women in every historical epoch and community musical experience is, in ways which they cannot diagnose or verbalize, "transcendent." Music's otherwise inexpressible powers of signification appear to be the natural simulacrum of religious experience. Of experience "outside experience." With uttermost yet inexplicable obviousness, music initiates, communicates truths, emotions, imaginings beyond any empirical or mundane presence. Its light and shadow, its agencies of possession—so feared by Plato, by Lenin—are "on the other side" of analytic and discursive reason. Our immersion in music can in some modest yet authentic sense be qualified as "mystical." Associations between music on the one hand and with eros and death on the other are as intimate in Monteverdi or Schubert as they are in rap. Though religion has at certain historical moments of austerity sought to limit its impact, it draws copiously on the sensuous ministry of music. It has enlisted musical exultation and lament and their inference of creative realities beyond proof. Psychologists invoke an "oceanic feeling," which music can induce and disseminate like no other human phenomenon. To so many of us this "oceanic feeling" stands more or less consciously for religious assent and elevation. A "surpassing" of this order may serve manifest doctrine as it does in Bach or all manner of diffuse but penetrating intimations. Exemplary of these, almost meretriciously so, are the adagios of Mahler. But no Bach chorale, no Bruckner fanfare, transport us as it may, has any evidence to offer as to the existence or nonexistence of a god. It has nothing to say on the matter.

Perhaps dance comes nearest to felt mystery. David dances before the Ark; the Dervish whirls; Nietzsche hints hauntingly at the translation of metaphysical thought and perception into dance, at the "dancing of truth"; Hindu deities are shown dancing. Again, no evidence is forthcoming.

What I have argued from my very first books onward, from *Tolstoy or Dostoevsky* and *The Death of Tragedy*, what I have tried to teach is this: It has been the "God question," that of God's existence or nonexistence and the attempts to give to this existence "a habitation and a name," which until very recently have fueled much of great art, literature, and speculative constructs. They have provided consciousness with its center.

Incised in the human psyche, possibly instrumental in our evolution, a hunger for supernatural reinsurance, for divine custodianship, whether consoling or punitive, loving or enraged, has informed human sensibility when it is at serious play. Faith makes endurable and challenging what would otherwise be an insensate solitude. Mythologies, without whose narratives and allegories of manifold meanings the imagination would be destitute, are the colloquialism of religion. We cannot conceive of an inward or outward secularism in any absolute sense. Of bordering on nothingness (though it is Heidegger's force to adumbrate this circumscription). It is a banality, though not one always attended to, to acknowledge the postulates of transcendence which have generated and underwritten our arts from Cro-Magnon cave paintings to Matisse's chapel at Vence, from Gregorian chant to Schoenberg, from *Gilgamesh* and Aeschylus to Dostoevsky and T. S. Eliot. In essence, *poiesis,* creation has been an *imitatio* of, a wrestling with what is taken to be divine making. "Let there be" urge the artist and the thinker in mimicry of a primal begetting. We ache for encounter with the gods via what Rilke called the terror and strangeness of beauty, a concept undefined as is that of the preternatural.

Should that ache cease, should the hunger at the heart of us ebb from adult need and vitality (as it does, prophetically, in Matthew Arnold's "Dover Beach"), certain magnitudes in poetics, philosophical discourse, and the arts would, I intuit, recede also. Like galaxies slipping over "the edge" into inertness. More and more, the "otherworldly" dimensions, the openendedness toward blinding light or devouring darkness would be out of reach. But without these there could have been no book of Job, no *Oresteia,* no *Commedia,* or *King Lear,* no *Missa Solemnis.* Nor indeed could there have been such immanent totalities as Goya's etchings or Proust's fiction. The "great stories" will gather respectful dust as do the tape recordings in our sound archives. Atheist poetry of stature has been exceedingly rare, though we do find it in, say, Leopardi, Shelley or Rimbaud. I am unable to attach tangible meaning to the concept of atheist music. What would, in the absence of transcendental eventuality, distinguish metaphysics from empirical psychology or the history of ideas? It does look as if we are at present in a phase of confusion and intermittence prior to as yet opaque metamorphoses. Of this transition, a genius such as that of Beckett would be representative.

But let there be no self-deception. Indispensable as they have been to our humanity, wondrous as they are in respect to human ascent, neither the arts nor philosophy, neither the Sistine Chapel nor Kant's *Critiques* solve the problem of whether God is or is not. They may have everything to tell us of a waiting for Godot. They tell us nothing of His arrival. And the night is getting long.

Enter theology and its bodyguard, theodicy, the justification of God's ways to man. A pursuit which has, century after century, bred "monuments of unageing intellect." Endless millions of earnest words. Myths, fables, visions, revelations, tractates, compendious systems, disputations, treatises, prose and poetry without end. Ranging across every category of rapture, of affirmation, of witness and analysis. Mountains of script and print higher than any tower. In what spheres of persuasion and of contoversy have there been more strenuous acrobatics of logic, more jubilant epiphanies, more fierce critiques and maledictions, a denser compaction of learning, meditations more sustained, confessions more naked than in theological arguments on God? Summits of the mind in Plato's teachings on the supreme good, in Aristotle's doctrine of the unmoved mover, in Augustine's trinitarian demonstrations, in Aquinas's *Summa* or Descartes's ontological proof. A matchless exposition of human infirmity in Pascal, in Kierkegaard, or in Karl Barth on *Romans*. Not to speak of the teeming wealth of Hebraic, Islamic, and Far Eastern theologies and theosophies. Prodigal and inspired "grammars of assent" to use Newman's subtle rubric. Take away the millennial debates on divine foreknowledge and Providence, on original sin and redemption, on creation everlasting or ex nihilo; cancel out Talmudic and Scholastic analytics and their modulation into metaphor; efface Persian mysticism or Chinese cosmologies—and how barren is the landscape. Talking about the gods seems to be a compulsion grounded in man's guts.

The intellectual energies, the acuities of feeling invested in seeking to prove the existence of a god are awesome. Those whom they have persuaded are legion and count among them the best qualified. Generations have felt reassured (or terrified). Millions, hundreds of millions proclaim the self-evidence of Allah. *Credo in unum Deo* professes Judeo-Christianity.

Yet do any of these demonstrations leap beyond the terms in which they are couched? Can they ever bound across their own shadow? The ingenuity of Anselm's ontological proof—God's perfection necessarily entails His existence—is transparently circular (early critics, soon silenced, saw this). Descartes's seductive contention that man's unaided intellect could not have conceived of infinity falls prey to the simple insight that our notion of "the infinite" is an extension of our awareness of very large sizes, of continuous series. Arguments from design as in the deism of the Enlightenment must construe a primitive analogy between the cosmos and watchmaking. They have been refuted, albeit not totally, by Darwinism and astrophysics. It is more than plausible that we have created the gods in our own rudimentary image. We seem to be "wired" to submit to, to rebel against the *Magna Mater,* or that angry volcanic father on Mount Sinai or four-armed Kali. The fear of being orphaned in existential emptiness, of being annihilated by death, of randomness, seems to have been more unbearable than the inventions of a world under supernatural surveillance, even if it is thronged with demonic agencies.

But the fact remains: words end in words. Pictures are pictures. There can be no passwords to the beyond. As Gorgias the irrefutable logician showed, there can be no proposition that does not entail the obverse of its own negation. Or, as Kant and Wittgenstein teach us, though with scrupulous sadness, attempts to demonstrate God's existence via reasoned arguments, via human discourse, are doomed to absurdity. Strictly considered, all theology, however profound or eloquent, is verbiage.

The frustrations of theodicy are even bleaker. Numberless are those, and again they comprise the most sagacious and inspired among us, who have striven to make understandable man's suffering under God. To render acceptable the bestialities and injustice of reality. No dilemma has elicited more anguished findings and therapeutic fantastications than that of unmerited suffering. The psychological insights, the virtuosities of rhetoric—as these pirouette above the abyss—are boundless. The catalogue of apologia runs on and on. Suffering is the necessary condition of human freedom, of the privileges of free will. Men and women are innately, hereditarily culpable, branded by their fall from some state of Edenic grace, but susceptible, *o felix culpa,* to salvation, to messianic redemption. How could there be forgiveness without sin? Those who endure injustice, enslavement, infirmity in this life will be compensated in the next. What seems outrageous, undeserved *misère* to our limited souls is only a minute particle of an all-encompassing, benevolent design intelligible solely to the deity and to be revealed only at the last apocalyptic hour. Pain, loss, humiliation are therapeutic; they draw forth what is best in us. Over time, the sum of the good, of reward, vastly exceeds that of torment and deprivation. Who is Job, who are we, to complain, to demand intelligible equity on the minute, risible ash heap of our brief lives? This plea bargaining has persisted across the millennia.

How far does it get us? Long before Dostoevsky there were those who demanded to know whether the torture of a single child, whether the death by hunger of a single crippled child did not refute the very concept of a just, compassionate God. What justifies the birth of a human being diminished, maddened by some genetic defect? What conceivable rationale, let alone morality, attaches to the interminable sequence of natural disasters, plague, famine, massacre which we call "history"? Why Socrates waffles the challenge—does the despot, the depraved, the sadist flourish when decent women and men are mocked and pounded to dust? What honesty, what moral disgust makes of suicide "the only serious philosophic question"(Camus)? Posed with more or less stringency, at greater or lesser personal risk, these questions are or ought to be commonplace.

The atrocities of the twentieth century have given them a new edge. The programmed torture, the murder of millions of blameless men, women and children; the incineration in planned firestorms of entire cities; the burial alive of thousands in "killing fields"; the coexistence, at close quarters, of unbridled material ostentation and homicidal poverty, hunger, and disease; the economic and sexual exploitation of children on an unprecedented scale—these have once again exposed the mendacities, the hollowness of theodicies. I had, for a considerable time, clung to conjectures that God was in some mode of recession, of "tiredness," and that He required man's collaboration; or that He was "not yet," that He was only coming into being. Now such tropes seem to me more or less fatuous. They belong to the entrancing melodrama inherent in language. On the third day of the Chechen seizure of the school in Beslan, the children were dying of torturing thirst. Even their urine had ceased. For two days, they had prayed to almighty God. No reply. On the final day, they called for help to Harry Potter and his favorite Wizard. This seems to me as close as we can get to the truth of the human situation. It has far greater dignity than the often repellent efforts to show the ultimate benevolence, the justice of "God after Auschwitz." A cold disgust overcomes one at the assurance that men's sinfulness and disobedience to divine commandments have brought on retribution (instances of this rabbinic cant were heard at the doors to the gas ovens). Words, words, words on the one hand, interminably eloquent and ingenuous; the scream of the suffocating child, of the tortured, of those dying from avoidable diseases and starvation on the other. And the bottomless reservoir of fanatical hatred from within organized religions themselves. Sectarian massacres have again become the order of the day. Have there ever been atheist mobs?

The idea that I should have anything original, let alone authoritative to offer in reply has always struck me as an impertinence. My understanding, my brain are wholly inadequate to the task. This may be the crux. If there should be any substance, any "truth-function" correspondent to what we refer to as "God," these would be of an order and composition inaccessible to our grasp and to any idiom in which such a grasp is inevitably formulated. We would not know what it is we are talking about. A deity commensurate with any of our abstract definitions, with any of our symbolic and metaphoric paraphrases would hardly be worth worshipping. Such a "God" would be as anthropomorphic as are the pictures our painters have made of Him, as pathetically human as are the statues carved of Him. Even the ascetic circumloctutions and abstentions from concreteness of a Spinoza—there are none purer—do not transcend our stuttering or the pathos of reason. To believe that we can somehow enfold "God" in our mental and emotional compass is to inhabit a house of mirrors. This is not "negative mystique." Primary questions in the natural sciences, in mathematics look to be beyond any means of solution. We are empowered to ask more and more pointed questions as to the origins of our cosmos, as to its possible end, as to the likelihood that there are millions of other "universes." We can juggle with attributes of time and its inception. These do not provide certitudes greater than the audacities of Saint Augustine. Hypotheses will remain hypotheses. It is the marvel of the human cortex, so small, so bounded an instrument, that it can pose unanswerable questions, that it can energize the undecidable and the insoluble. It is this paradox, this sense of unbounded limitation which fills me with awe, this sense of the overwhelming unknowns of the everyday. It is every moment of examined existence, not any inconceivable or impotent deity, which abides our question. We are the creature which will not stop asking and getting it wrong.

Feeble, provisional as they are, I cherish intuitions by which I have tried to live more or less sanely. The social thinker, Max Horkheimer, called the concept of original sin the most seminal insight ever fostered by men. Only the fundamentalist, only the "literalist" will regard it as factual, as anything but myth. On any historical, anthropological level it makes no sense other than that, so often fathomless, to be found in fairy tales. The notion of inherited primordial guilt is morally revolting. Yet I cannot help making out, without being able to explain it, the intimation, the remembrance of some initial catastrophe. Something went terribly wrong at the outset. Buried somewhere in the magma of the unconscious are traces of such disaster—a word which has in it the fall of the stars—memories unrecapturable to memory. It is as if we had been or become an unwelcome guest in creation. As if being had not made us welcome. This might account for the suicidal rage with which we now ravage our planet, with which we strive to eradicate the last and accusing vestiges of the Edenic. Some irretrievable recollection light years, or rather "dark years," away presses on us. This intimation does not justify human suffering in any rational vein, it does not validate the recurrent defeat of moral ideals. But as great teachers of sadness have seen, it does allow one to get on with living. To "fail, fail again, then fail better" (Beckett). Although that too may be too sanguine.

I am haunted, to the point of panic, by the fragility of reason. At virtually any moment a physical lesion, a drug, processes of ageing can impair or destroy our reason. The child born mentally handicapped, the aged companion babbling because of Alzheimer's disease, frame the miraculous complexity and good fortune of rationality. It is these which inhibit me from regarding as plausible the existence of a "God" along human lines. Not to speak of a deity attending to our minuscule hopes and anguish in the trillion-fold matter of a local universe. Organized religion can infect reason, can twist it to madness. How many pogroms in the name of a loving Christ, how many pilgrims mauled to death in Mecca, how endless the slaughter over puerile details of ritual or legend! The chanting, gyrating Orthodox Jew, a virtuosos of detestations, the Christian at his genuflections, the salaaming Muslim are testimony to the slow, wasteful prehistory of common sense. Whether in prayer or in theological theses, pronouncements about the will and attributes of God are self-fulfilling tautologies. Unlike those of algebra or of formal logic, they summon immense strengths of feeling. But so do sex or hunger or greed.

What I have come to feel with compelling intensity is the absence of God. Not in the rather sophistic sense of negative theology, of a *Deus absconditus*. I do not suppose that I can put this feeling into intelligible words. The creation of a vacuum produces implosive pressures so great they can tear anything apart. The emptiness I feel has enormous power. It confronts me with ethical, with intellectual demands beyond any I can satisfy. It is—and I know that this is only a sort of mumbling—a nihilism brimful with the unknown. It reduces my apprehension of existence, my pitiful attempts to conceptualize death, to the confines of my mind and consciousness—a very small space. But this feeling will not let me bluff. It relates, and again words fail me, to the sadness, to the abyss at the heart of love. Perhaps it is something like the animate dark in which a blind man taps his way through the world's illusory noon. Meditation on a "non-God" can be as concentrated, as humble or exultant as any in approved theology and worship. It does not, I believe, trigger folly and hatred. Awesome is the God who is not.

What I would advance fervently is this: faith or the lack thereof is or ought to be the most private, the most discreetly guarded constitutent of the human person. The soul, too, must have its private parts. Publication cheapens and falsifies belief irremediably. The adult believer seeks to be alone with his God. As I strive to be with His sovereign absence. Already I have said, I have failed to say, too much.

An ancient curse has it: "May mine enemy publish a book." To which I now add: "May he publish seven."